THE
INFOGRAPHIC
GUIDE TO
THE BIBLE:
THE OLD TESTAMENT

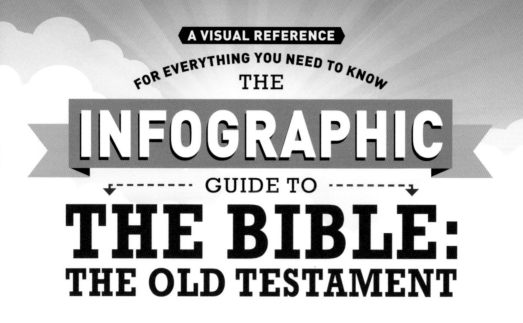

A VISUAL REFERENCE
FOR EVERYTHING YOU NEED TO KNOW
THE
INFOGRAPHIC
GUIDE TO
THE BIBLE:
THE OLD TESTAMENT

HILLARY THOMPSON;
THE REV. EDWARD F. DUFFY, PhD; and ERIN DAWSON

Adams Media
New York   London   Toronto   Sydney   New Delhi

Adams Media
An Imprint of Simon & Schuster, LLC
100 Technology Center Drive
Stoughton, Massachusetts 02072

First Adams Media trade paperback edition NOVEMBER 2017

ADAMS MEDIA and colophon are trademarks of Simon and Schuster.

For information about special discounts for bulk purchases, please contact Simon & Schuster Special Sales at 1-866-506-1949 or business@simonandschuster.com.

The Simon & Schuster Speakers Bureau can bring authors to your live event. For more information or to book an event contact the Simon & Schuster Speakers Bureau at 1-866-248-3049 or visit our website at www.simonspeakers.com.

Interior design by Erin Dawson
Interior images © Shutterstock, iStockphoto.com, Getty Images, and 123RF

Printed by Versa Press, Inc., East Peoria, IL, U.S.A.

10 9 8 7

ISBN 978-1-5072-0487-0
ISBN 978-1-5072-0488-7 (ebook)

Scripture quotations are from the Holy Bible, King James Version.

Contents

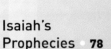

INTRODUCTION

The Bible is the most-read book in the world. The first half of this meaningful and substantial book, the Old Testament, is crucial for understanding the foundation of the Abrahamic religions and the relationship God had with the Israelites. But sitting down to read through every chapter, story, and verse can be a challenge for anyone, from religious leaders to laypeople. And deciphering some of the most cryptic text—like so much found in the Old Testament—can be a demanding task without historical context, knowledge of religious terminology, and most importantly, time. That's where *The Infographic Guide to the Bible: The Old Testament* comes in.

This set of fifty colorful, easy-to-reference infographics offers detailed explanations of some of the most important concepts, stories, and characters the Old Testament presents. Whether you're looking to supplement your Bible study, find a quick and easy reference for a religious education course, or simply brush up on Old Testament facts, this handy guide covers a broad range of topics in comprehensive yet concise charts, lists, and graphs.

With this guide to the Old Testament, you'll learn about key events in biblical history, including the timeline of creation, the flood, and Israel's exodus from slavery. Essential concepts are discussed, like the Ten Commandments, God's covenant with Israel, and the holy festivals of Israel. You'll find facts about the Old Testament's most famous and influential people, including Abraham, Noah, Moses, Ruth, David, Jacob, and Esther. Visual representations highlight some of the biggest Old Testament stories, like the Tower of Babel, David and Goliath, and Daniel in the Lions' Den. You'll also discover central yet lesser-known characters, like the prophet Malachi, uncover the important roles women played in upholding the Lord's commands, and witness the Lord's wrath during the ten plagues of Egypt.

From the story of Adam and Eve to decoding the prophets' predictions of the coming of the Messiah, Jesus Christ, *The Infographic Guide to the Bible: The Old Testament* is a wide-ranging resource presenting the Old Testament in a fresh, new format.

GENESIS:
A Timeline of Creation

The first chapter of the first book of the Bible, Genesis, tells the story of God's creation of the world in a chronological sequence of six days. Even in the early Christian church, great thinkers debated whether this meant six calendar days, or rather six aeons, or periods of time. Genesis 2 offers a complementary

IN THE BEGINNING

"In the beginning God created the heaven and the earth." (Genesis 1:1) At the beginning of time, the world was without light or form, but the Spirit of God was everywhere. Did God create everything ("the heaven and the earth") out of nothing (*ex nihilo*), or rather out of pre-existing matter ("the earth was without form")?

SECOND DAY

On the second day, God created the heavens. He separated these from the earthly world. Genesis says that each of the acts of creation was "good." There is no "dualism"—as if heaven were created "good," and the earth, "evil." It was all "good."

FIRST DAY

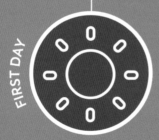

On the first day, God created light (the day), and separated it from darkness (the night). In this first act of creation, we notice a pattern. Everything comes about by God's Word: "Let there be light: and there was light."

THIRD DAY

The third day brought about dry land, called Earth, which yielded grass, herbs, seeds, and trees bearing fruit. God gathered all of the waters together to form the seas.

version of the creation story—not with the chronological flow of the first chapter, but with a more focused theme of the creation of humankind. Both chapters set the foundation for much of the scripture that will follow. Consider the first account of creation, in Genesis 1:1–2:4. Over the course of seven days, God shapes the world from a dark and desolate place to a planet teeming with life and light, and filled with His love.

SIXTH DAY

On the sixth day, God created all animals that live on land, from tiny insects to the largest mammals. He also created mankind on this day, in His image and likeness. God gave mankind the power to rule over the world and all its inhabitants, and deemed men and women good. While the creation of humankind is the crown of creation, we can see that God's creation is not totally focused on people. Mankind will have "dominion" in such a way that we are to be stewards of everything else that has been created—to take care of the creation, and not exploit it.

On the fourth day, God created all of the heavenly bodies: the stars, the sun, and the moon. He did this so people could track time, and to give light to the day and divide it from the night.

FOURTH DAY

God created life on the fifth day—life for animals that live in the water or fly through the air. God created all birds, along with whales and other creatures that thrive in the seas. He blessed these creatures, so they could multiply across the earth.

FIFTH DAY

SEVENTH DAY

God rested on the seventh day, as the heavens and earth were finished. He blessed and sanctified this day, and established the rule of keeping one day of rest during the week. "Rest" is understood to mean not just "relaxation" but actually "resting in" God— deep trust and undivided fellowship with God.

God created Adam, and placed him in the Garden of Eden to take care of it. Although Adam was surrounded by animals, God did not want Adam to be alone.

This phrase brings out a great truth in scripture, namely that people were created for relationships, with one another, and with their Creator.

God placed Adam in a deep sleep, took a rib from him, and created Eve as his partner, "bone of my bones, and flesh of my flesh." (Genesis 2:23)

It is unlikely that the scripture intends to say that we should not know good from evil or right from wrong, but rather that we should not know these things *apart from God*. God intends for us to live in undivided fellowship with our Creator.

Adam and Eve felt shame for the first time, and hid from the Lord in fear of punishment. God cursed them for their disobedience.

ADAM and EVE and
Original Sin

In the second creation narrative, God creates Adam from dust and Eve from one of Adam's ribs. Together they live in the Garden of Eden, and God instructs them to care for the garden and all the life within it. Though God forbids them from eating from the tree of knowledge of good and evil, Satan nonetheless tempts them to eat from it. Their actions and punishment, traced here, illustrate the scriptural basis for Original Sin and man's fall from grace, central themes in Christianity and the Bible.

Both Adam and Eve were naked, but were not ashamed because they lived in the favor of the Lord and followed His Word.

Adam and Eve could eat from any tree in the garden, except for the tree of knowledge of good and evil.

Disobeying God's rule (even just *touching* the tree!) would result in death for Adam and Eve.

Eve refused at first, fearing God's Word.

Temptation came from Satan, who appeared in the form of a snake. *Satan* literally means "the one who obstructs," or "the accuser." He enticed Eve to eat from the tree.

Once Eve saw that the fruit of the tree was good, she took a piece to eat, and gave one to Adam as well. Satan convinced her that by eating from the tree, they would be like God, knowing good and evil.

Recognizing their nakedness, Adam and Eve clothed themselves.

God banished Adam and Eve from the Garden of Eden. God also cursed the serpent, and the ground upon which Adam and Eve stood.

The story of this first sin offers a basis for understanding the struggles and challenges humanity will face, both in the stories of the Bible and in their own lives. It is a framework for understanding the realities of being human, or why and how things are the way they are (aetiology): like the knowledge of our own mortality, endless labor, shame and blame, painful childbirth, the need for clothing, and the nature of sin.

Adam's Genealogy:
THE ORIGINAL FAMILY TREE

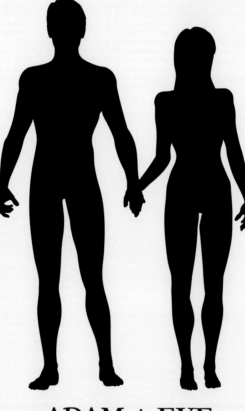

ADAM + EVE

The genealogies in the Old Testament are a way for the writers of scripture to tell us that everyone whom the Lord has made is *valued* and remembered. The first book of the Bible, Genesis, describes the genealogies of the first generations of people created by the Lord. First, the Lord made Adam, and made him a wife, Eve, from Adam's rib. Their children would bring forth the next generations to serve the Lord. This flow chart visualizes the descendants of Adam and Eve, all the way to Noah and the time of the flood.

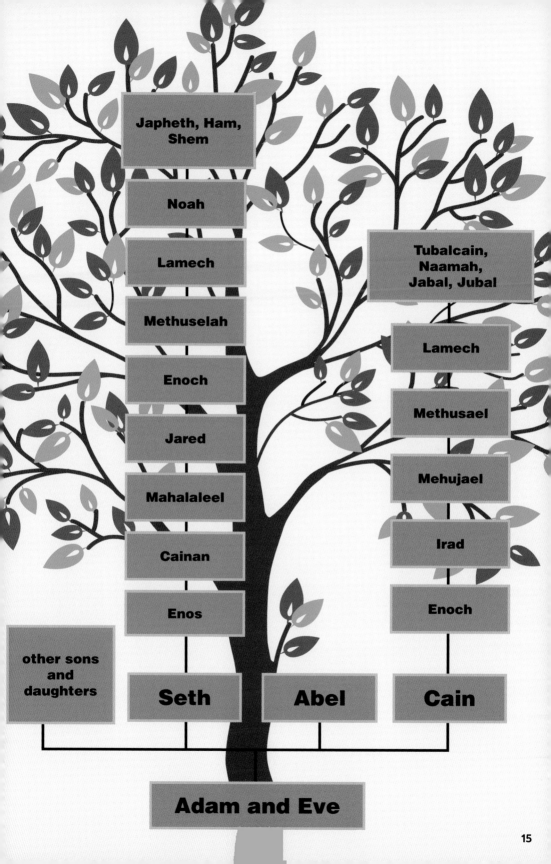

Japheth, Ham, Shem

Noah

Lamech

Methuselah

Enoch

Jared

Mahalaleel

Cainan

Enos

other sons and daughters

Seth

Abel

Tubalcain, Naamah, Jabal, Jubal

Lamech

Methusael

Mehujael

Irad

Enoch

Cain

Adam and Eve

CAIN VERSUS ABEL:

A STRUGGLE TO PLEASE THE LORD

Cain and Abel were the sons of Adam and Eve—Cain the eldest and Abel the younger brother. Granted different skill sets and abilities, Cain perceives the Lord to favor Abel, and as such grows jealous of his younger brother. Though Abel pays the ultimate sacrifice for his brother's jealousy, through Cain's story readers can learn the true meaning of giving, and of obeying the Lord's Word.

CAIN was a farmer, and he tilled the soil to grow crops.

ABEL was a skilled shepherd, and tended a flock of sheep.

Cain brought a sacrifice of his farming, "the fruit of the ground," to offer to the Lord.

Following in his brother's footsteps, Abel offered a sacrifice to God, a first-born lamb. God respected Abel, and his offering, and praised him for it.

Because the Lord favored Abel's sacrifice, and not Cain's, Cain became angry, disheartened, and jealous of his younger brother.

Cain talked with Abel and led him to a field. There, Cain killed his brother.

The Lord cried out to Cain, asking where Abel had gone. Cain answered with the infamous lie, "I know not: Am I my brother's keeper?" (Genesis 4:9)

God cursed Cain for killing his brother: Cain would no longer be able to farm, and the Lord banished him to walk the world alone. Despite this punishment, He offered mercy by placing a mark on Cain, so no other man would kill him.

Cain settled in the land of Nod, where he took a wife, built a city, and had children.

Though this story does not explain *why* God favored Abel's sacrifice over Cain's, it does seem to invite us to ponder that question deeply. Did God favor Abel's offering because Cain was filled with resentment? (God always looks at the attitude of the heart, not just our outward sacrifice.) Or was it that Abel somehow had given the best he had to offer (costly—not cheap—giving)? Or does the story just point to the fact that God is sovereign and chooses whom He will choose, and when?

BABEL:
THE UNFINISHED TOWER

The Tower of Babel story is told in **Genesis 11,** and describes a central theme of the Bible: one cannot be fruitful *and* godless. In the time after the flood, Noah's descendants were living together and speaking the same language. They began to build a tower to reach heaven, so they wouldn't need God to get there, but God quickly put a stop to this. In a small number of verses, the Tower of Babel story emphasizes the importance of obeying God's Word.

At one time, there was only one language spoken by all the people of the world. Those people attempted to build a tower that would reach heaven —so they wouldn't need God to get there.

1 Language

1 People

The Lord scattered the people across the whole world in order to prevent pride, arrogance, and evil from spreading.

30 Languages
for the descendants of Ham

27 Languages
for the descendents of Shem

15 Languages
for the descendents of Japheth

72 Languages

As a result, the scattered people began speaking different languages. It's believed that a new language was created for the descendants of each of Noah's sons, resulting in seventy-two different languages.

Babel means "confusion," which is why the tower was given this name. When the people could not understand each other, they scattered across the land.

NOAH'S ARK:
BY THE NUMBERS

Noah's Ark is one of the most popular stories in the Old Testament. It is found in **Genesis 6–8.** The flood narrative starts during a time of great evil in the world. All the people had come to disregard the Lord's Word; their thoughts and actions were carried out in evil and sin. However, God favored the righteous Noah and his family. The Lord instructed Noah to build an ark to shelter his family, and bring aboard two of every creature, to protect them from the rains and floods brought about to destroy the world's evil inhabitants. Building and stocking such an ark was a major task, but it was designed to withstand the full year of the flood, as shown here.

ARK COMPONENTS

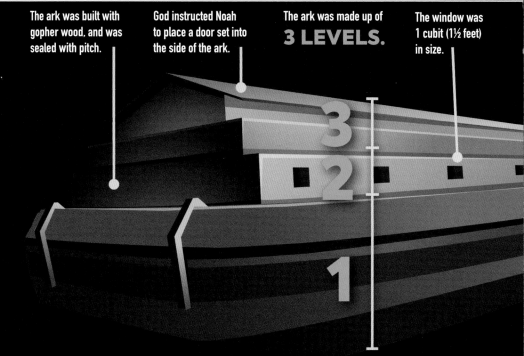

The ark was built with gopher wood, and was sealed with pitch.

God instructed Noah to place a door set into the side of the ark.

The ark was made up of **3 LEVELS.**

The window was 1 cubit (1½ feet) in size.

ARK MEASUREMENTS

300 cubits long × **50** cubits wide × **30** cubits high

1 CUBIT = 1½ feet or 18 inches

450 feet long × **75** feet wide × **45** feet high

1,518,750 CUBIC FEET

ARK INHABITANTS

Noah and his wife; Noah's sons: Shem, Ham, Japheth, and their wives

Noah was **600** years old!

2 of every living creature on earth, male and female: the fowl, cattle, and "creeping things." Some of the largest estimates claim there were more than **7,500** species, or upwards of **16,000** animals on board!

- Clean beasts were brought on board by sevens.
- Unclean beasts were brought on board by twos.

The waters rose **15 CUBITS** (22½ feet) across the earth.

Noah was instructed to gather "all the food that is eaten," and bring enough to feed his family and all of the animals on the ark.

---

70 days after the flood ends, Noah leaves the ark.

14 days after the flood ends, Noah opens the door.

FLOOD ENDS

23 Dove leaves again; days later the flood ends.

Noah sends another dove (**7** days later). It returns with an olive leaf.

40 days later, Noah opens the ark door. Noah sends a raven and a dove to check for dry land. They return after 7 days and report that the flood waters have not yet receded.

For **73** days, the waters begin to recede. On the 73rd day, the mountains reappear.

The ark stops and rests.

150TH DAY

The waters continue to rise for another **110** days.

It rains for **40** days and **40** nights. On the 40th day, the ark floats.

DAYS 1–40

DAY 1 OF FLOOD

START

For **7** days Noah loads animals onto the ark.

God tells Noah to board the ark.

21

ABRAHAM: PATRIARCH OF JUDAISM

Abraham is the first patriarch of Judaism, and he is held in high esteem in Christianity and Islam as well. He is known as the founder of the covenant, the first unconditional promise God made to mankind. God promises land for Abraham's descendants and perhaps most importantly, promises blessings and redemption for the people of Israel.

> 66 Behold, my covenant is with thee, and thou shalt be a father of many nations...thy name shall be **Abraham.** 99
>
> Genesis 17:4–5

Establishing the Covenant

When Abraham was ninety-nine, the Lord came to Abraham and made a covenant with him. God declared that Abraham would be the founder of many nations.

1 Before this moment, Abraham was known as Abram. God decreed that he change his name to Abraham. His wife, Sarai, would be known as Sarah. The change of names indicates their changed relationship with God—as they are now in covenant with the Lord. The meaning of their new names also explains their new mission: Abraham (father of many); Sarah (princess of many).

2 Abraham would be fruitful, and would receive the fruit of three specific promises: land, being the father of a great nation, and Israel becoming a blessing to all nations.

3 God warned Abraham of the Israelites' impending slavery in Egypt.

4 God commanded Abraham to keep His covenant sacred, and to keep it with future generations.

5 Abraham and his male descendants would be circumcised.

6 The Lord also established the covenant with Isaac, Abraham and Sarah's son, who would be born a year after the covenant was made.

Sacrificing Isaac

Abraham was **100 YEARS OLD** when his son Isaac was born!

Even though she was elderly, Sarah gave birth to Isaac **ONE YEAR** after the covenant was made, just as God promised.

God commanded Abraham to offer Isaac as a sacrifice to Him, to test his faith and devotion to the Lord. Abraham and Isaac traveled **THREE DAYS** to the sacrificial mountain in Moriah.

Abraham complied, but just as he was about to kill Isaac, the angel of the Lord revealed a ram caught in a thicket by his horns. Abraham sacrificed the ram instead of Isaac. This was the **2ND TIME** the angel of the Lord called down to him.

Founding Religions

The major "Abrahamic religions" that trace their origins to Abraham are:

7TH CENTURY B.C.
JUDAISM
(or earlier)

1ST CENTURY A.D.
CHRISTIANITY

7TH CENTURY A.D.
ISLAM

Worldwide Religions

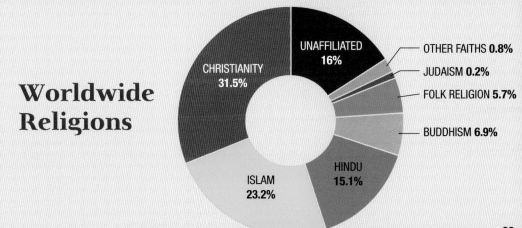

- CHRISTIANITY 31.5%
- UNAFFILIATED 16%
- OTHER FAITHS 0.8%
- JUDAISM 0.2%
- FOLK RELIGION 5.7%
- BUDDHISM 6.9%
- HINDU 15.1%
- ISLAM 23.2%

SARAH:
MOTHER OF NATIONS

Sarah is a matriarch of the Old Testament and of Judaism. The wife of Abraham, she was chosen by God to be "the mother of nations," for her descendants would form the line of Jesus, the Messiah (the genealogy of Jesus is given at the start of Matthew's gospel, Chapter 1). By bearing Abraham's son, she upheld the Lord's covenant with Abraham, ensuring Abraham would be the founder of many nations to come.

> " I will bless her, and she shall be a mother of nations; kings of people shall be of her."
>
> (GENESIS 17:16)

A NAME CHANGE

God changed Sarah's original name, just as He did with Abraham. *Sarai*, meaning "my princess," was changed to *Sarah*, meaning "princess." The slight alteration represents the fact that Sarah would become matriarch for *all*—thereby mirroring God's plan for Israel itself to be a blessing to all nations. (Genesis 18:18)

THE BONDSWOMAN

For most of her life, Sarah could not conceive a child with her husband, Abraham. Although the Lord promised Sarah she would have a child, she feared she could never conceive. Because she did not want Abraham to live without an heir, Sarah allowed her Egyptian servant, Hagar, to lie with Abraham. Hagar conceived a son, Ishmael, who grew to have a strong relationship with his father. Hagar grew to despise Sarah, and Sarah in return treated Hagar with contempt. Genesis is frank about Sarah and Abraham's scheme to preserve, by their human ingenuity, God's plan for them to have descendants, when they could not, humanly, see how it would come about. Yet it actually could not have pleased the Lord—after all, they did not trust unconditionally in His promise. When the messengers told Abraham that Sarah would have a child, she "laughed." (Genesis 18:12)

10 years

Hagar lived with Sarah and Abraham for ten years before she conceived Ishmael.

90 years

Because Sarah ignored the Lord's promise, she had to wait until she was ninety years old to conceive her son, Isaac.

4,000 years

Some trace modern conflicts between people of Muslim and Jewish faiths 4,000 years back to the rift between Sarah and Hagar. Muslims trace their lineage and faith back through Ishmael, and Jews trace their lineage back through Isaac.

7

TAKEAWAYS

— FROM —

SODOM

— AND —

GOMORRAH

GENESIS 18-19 tells the narrative of the cities of Sodom and Gomorrah, and the grievous sins their people committed against the Lord. In this story, three angels disguised as men visited Abraham, the founder of Israel and God's chosen one. Genesis does not explain exactly what happened at Sodom and Gomorrah; it simply states the people were sinning against God, and reveals what happened to them—the consequences for their actions. Though the outcome was grim for these people (God rained fire and brimstone down upon them), there are several important lessons you can draw from the narrative, to develop deeper trust in God.

RECOGNIZE AND ACKNOWLEDGE THE SINS AROUND YOU; DO NOT IGNORE THEM. Lot, Abraham's nephew, lived among the people of Sodom, and allowed them to influence his actions and his family. By accepting their sins, rather than standing against them, Lot came dangerously close to succumbing to them. This is the danger of syncretism (the blending of two or more religions)—a recurring theme in the Old Testament.

AVOID EXCESSIVE PRIDE AND ARROGANCE. Sodom and Gomorrah are notorious for sexual sins. But their inhabitants were also described as prideful and arrogant people—they did not think sinning against God was shameful. By being cognizant of the presence of pride and arrogance in the world, you can take action to stay humble and respectful of God's Word and the people around you.

TAKE CARE OF YOUR FELLOW MAN. The people of Sodom and Gomorrah were consumed by selfishness. They possessed an abundance of food and wealth (remember: Lot had chosen this region in the first place because it was more fertile), but they neglected the poor and suffering among them. (Ezekiel 16:49) Be sure to recognize those struggling in your own life and community, and do not be afraid to offer aid or assistance—no matter how small your gesture might be.

BEWARE THE TEMPTATION AND INFLUENCE OF OTHERS. Lot was swayed by the actions and sins of the Sodomites. He even offered his daughters to them as a sacrifice. Abraham was able to step in and turn Lot away from sin and back to following the Lord's Word. The modern world offers temptations that can pull you away from God. These range from excessive greed to jealousy of others. Remembering this story can heighten your awareness of these pulls, and give you the power to avoid them.

HEED WARNING SIGNS AS THEY APPEAR. We do this by having an "undivided heart" of faith in God. The Lord tells us to remember Lot's wife! The Lord told Lot and his family to flee for their lives as the cities were being destroyed. Though His message was clear, Lot's wife did not heed the warning: she turned to look back at the cities, and was changed into a pillar of salt. She was divided between following God and remaining with her people; her "being divided" or "distracted" led to her demise. Following simple signs and trusting God undividedly are the best ways to avoid spiritual danger.

VERBALIZE YOUR BELIEFS AND FEELINGS. Lot was hesitant (Genesis 19:15–16) to defend the Lord to the Sodomites. Do not be afraid to voice your beliefs and feelings, even if those around you disagree.

WELCOME AND HELP STRANGERS WHEN YOU CAN. You never know who you may be helping! Abraham welcomed three strangers in this story, and they turned out to be angels (one was the Lord!). In a New Testament commentary on this passage, we are even told that when we extend hospitality, we may be entertaining "angels unawares." (Hebrews 13:2) God praises those who extend a helping hand and have mercy for those in need.

ISAAC & REBEKAH:

An Old Testament Love Story

GENESIS 24 describes when Abraham reached old age, and his beloved wife Sarah had died. Desperate for his son, Isaac, to uphold the covenant with God (and become father to many peoples), Abraham turned to his home country, Mesopotamia, to find his son a wife. A servant made the journey for him, and returned with Rebekah to be the young bride. This story speaks to the power of God's love for His people, and confirms how His promises will always be fulfilled for those who believe.

THE 10 CAMELS TEST

Abraham ordered a servant to take ten camels to Nahor, in Mesopotamia, to find Isaac a bride. The servant devised a plan to find a woman worthy of his master's son. The servant would stand next to a well with his ten camels and ask the women drawing water to share a drink—with all of them.

5 Love Lessons

Taken directly, this story centers upon the foundation of Isaac and Rebekah's marriage. But the true love expressed through this story is God's love for His people, and their faith, love, and devotion to Him in turn.

1 The promise to Abraham. Even though Abraham feared his son would not marry, the Lord delivered Rebekah to him. Abraham received God's love when He upheld His promise.

2 The servant's faith in God. Despite an arduous journey, and the *immense* task of finding his master's son a wife, the servant had faith in his Lord that the right woman would find them.

The Damsel

Rebekah approached the well with a pitcher on her shoulder. Described as a fair damsel and a virgin, she offered the servant a drink when he asked, and labored to water the camels as well. (GENESIS 24:15-19)

The Earring

When the camels had finished, the servant rewarded Rebekah for her generosity. He offered her "a golden earring of half a shekel weight, and two bracelets for her hands of ten shekels weight of gold." (GENESIS 24:22)

The Agreement

The servant asked Rebekah for lodging, and her family welcomed him as one "blessed of the Lord." (GENESIS 24:31) The servant explained his mission, and Rebekah's family agreed to her becoming Isaac's wife, as the Lord intended. (GENESIS 24:51)

The Meeting

Isaac and Rebekah met at dusk, as her camel caravan approached. Isaac went out into the fields to meditate at the time of her arrival. Upon seeing Isaac, Rebekah covered herself with a veil. (GENESIS 24:63-65)

3 The family's approval. Considering this factor through a historical lens (where daughters were married off, often for a dowry), Rebekah's family welcomed a stranger into their home, listened to his message, and accepted his mission from God.

4 Rebekah's acceptance. Some say Rebekah answered God's calling to follow the servant into Isaac's arms. Although she had to leave her family and her home to travel abroad and marry a man she had never seen, she trusted in God. The Lord rewarded her with a loving marriage and children who would continue the lineage of Jesus.

5 Isaac and Rebekah's sons. Rebekah faced a time when she could not bear children. Isaac prayed for her, and through God's love and power, Rebekah conceived twin sons: Esau and Jacob. Jacob would become the father of Israel.

JACOB'S LINEAGE

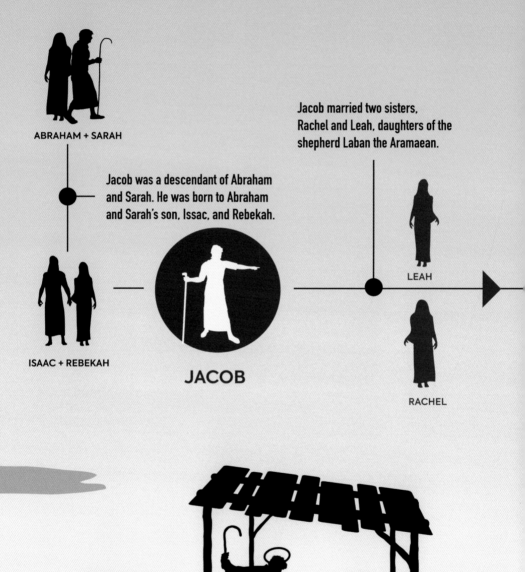

ABRAHAM + SARAH

Jacob was a descendant of Abraham and Sarah. He was born to Abraham and Sarah's son, Issac, and Rebekah.

Jacob married two sisters, Rachel and Leah, daughters of the shepherd Laban the Aramaean.

ISAAC + REBEKAH

JACOB

LEAH

RACHEL

An important patriarch of the Old Testament, Jacob was the son of Isaac and Rebekah, and grandson of Abraham. (GENESIS 25)

LEAH

JUDAH

Although Leah was not favored by Jacob, God quickly gave her four sons. Later Leah had three more children, including Jacob's only daughter.

BILHAH

Rachel could not conceive, so she offered her servant, Bilhah, to Jacob; they had two sons.

ZILPAH

Not wanting to be outdone, Leah gave Jacob her own servant, Zilpah, who also had two sons by him.

RACHEL

God then gave Rachel the ability to have children, and Jacob and Rachel had two sons.

Of these lines, King David would arise from the house of Judah (Leah), whose descendants would include the Messiah.

KING DAVID

Joseph the Dream Interpreter

Joseph, a significant figure in Genesis, had elaborate dreams that showed how he was favored by God. Over the course of his life, Joseph used dream interpretation to guide his path and deliver the Word of the Lord.

**Genesis 37:9–11
The Celestial Bodies**
Joseph dreamed the sun, moon, and stars bowed to him. When he told his father and siblings about the dream, his siblings began to plot to punish him.

=

**Genesis 37:3–8
The Sheaves**
Joseph dreamed he was binding grain into bundles, or sheaves, with his siblings. His sheaf stood upright while his siblings' sheaves bowed to it. His siblings took this to mean he would reign over them.

Genesis 37:3
Joseph was born to Jacob and Rachel; he was Jacob's favorite son.

Genesis 37:26–36
Joseph was sold into slavery by his jealous siblings.

Genesis 40:16–19, 22
The Chief Baker
= Joseph interpreted the Pharaoh's baker's dream of baskets of baked goods being eaten by birds to mean the Pharaoh would execute the baker and leave him outside to be consumed by birds.

Genesis 40:7–13, 21
The Chief Butler
= Joseph interpreted the Pharoah's butler's dream while they were in prison. The butler dreamed of a vine with three branches of grapes, which the butler squeezed into the Pharaoh's cup. Joseph correctly took it to mean the butler would be released in three days and given back his position.

Genesis 41:15–37
The Pharaoh
= Joseph interpreted the Pharaoh's dream of seven healthy cows eaten by seven skinny cows and seven healthy ears of corn eaten by seven skinny ears of corn to mean Egypt would experience seven years of a bountiful harvest followed by seven years of famine. His prophecy allowed Egypt to prepare for the coming years of famine.

Genesis 41:39–44

After his successful dream interpretations, the Pharaoh promoted Joseph from prisoner to advisor, the second most powerful position in Egypt.

MOSES:
PIVOTAL MOMENTS IN EXODUS

Moses, one of the most important prophets in the Bible, is known for delivering the Israelites out of slavery in Egypt. Moses is connected with many other stories that, taken collectively, form the complete picture of his life and his impact on the Abrahamic religions. Here, some of the best-known and most important moments are described and explained.

THE BABY BASKET

The Egyptian Pharaoh feared the Israelites would rise up against him and ordered that all Hebrew baby boys be killed. Moses' mother hid him in a basket by the Nile, where he was found by the Pharaoh's daughter, who raised him as her son. (EXODUS 2:1–10)

THE BURNING BUSH

Though raised as an Egyptian prince, Moses remembered his Hebrew roots. After killing an Egyptian who murdered an Israelite slave, Moses became a fugitive. During this time God, in the form of a burning bush, instructed Moses to return to Egypt and free the Israelites from slavery. (EXODUS 2:11–25, 3)

THE GOLDEN CALF

When Moses was on Mount Sinai, the Israelites created a false god in the form of a golden calf to worship. God informed Moses of the Israelites' sin and Moses returned and destroyed the calf, and called for the Israelites' repentance. (EXODUS 32)

THE ARK OF THE COVENANT

The Ark of the Covenant, a wooden chest gilded with gold, was created to house the Ten Commandments. The Ark was particularly sacred, as it served as a physical expression of the Lord on earth. (EXODUS 25)

ABOUT MOSES

- Name means "drew out of the water"
- Thought to have written five books of the Old Testament
- Known as the "Law Giver of Israel"
- Forbidden by God from entering the Promised Land
- Died at the age of 120

THE 10 COMMANDMENTS

After the Israelites crossed the Red Sea, God summoned Moses to the top of Mount Sinai and delivered the Ten Commandments. The Lord promised the Israelites that if they kept His commandments, He would go with them into the Promised Land. (EXODUS 20)

THE RED SEA

When Moses led the Israelites out of slavery they became trapped by the Pharaoh's army at the edge of the Red Sea. Moses lifted his rod over the waters, and the sea parted, allowing the Israelites safe passage across. Moses then raised his rod and closed the water, drowning the Pharaoh's army. (EXODUS 14)

Genesis 46 • Ezekiel 1

THROUGH VISIONS

God sometimes shows Himself through miraculous visions experienced by people, including Jacob and Ezekiel.

Amos 4

THROUGH THOUGHTS AND INTENTIONS

God often reveals His ways and intentions to us through our thoughts.

THEOPHANY:
REVEALING GOD

Throughout the Old Testament (and in the New), God appears to humankind in a variety of ways. These theophanies, or manifestations of God to human beings, are awe-inspiring incidents for those fortunate ones with whom the Lord chooses to communicate. There are several ways the Lord appears to humankind in the Old Testament.

Exodus 3

THROUGH THE UNKNOWN

One of the best-known instances of God appearing to a mortal is the story of Moses on Mount Horeb. God appears to him in the form of a burning bush, (a bush that burns but is not consumed by the flames), and explains how he will deliver the people of Israel from slavery in Egypt.

Job 38

THROUGH NATURE

God speaks to man through forces of nature, such as when He reveals Himself to Job in the form of a whirlwind.

Judges 6

THROUGH ORDINARY OBJECTS

God also uses ordinary objects to speak to His people. The Lord speaks to Gideon again, this time in the form of a fleece shirt.

Genesis 16 • Judges 6

THROUGH ANGELS

The angel of the Lord appears to Hagar and tells her that she will have a son named Ishmael.

The angel of the Lord appears to Gideon, prompting fears of death—but God bids him peace.

Genesis 20 • Genesis 41 • Daniel 2

THROUGH DREAMS

The Lord often communicates through dreams, bringing good and bad news to people such as Abimelech, the Pharaoh, and Nebuchadnezzar.

Genesis 18 • Genesis 32

THROUGH HUMAN CONTACT

God often approaches Old Testament characters in human form, such as when He appears to Abraham in the form of three men, or when He wrestles Jacob (yes, really!) in the form of a stranger.

1. Water to Blood

God commanded Moses to tell Aaron to spoil all the waters in Egypt, and he did. As a result, for seven days, the rivers, streams, pools, ponds, and vessels turned to blood. "And the fish that was in the river died; and the river stank, and the Egyptians could not drink of the water of the river; and there was blood throughout all the land of Egypt." (Exodus 7:21)

2. Frogs

Aaron again corrupted the rivers and ponds of Egypt, and caused frogs to invade Egypt. And the frogs came up from the waters and into the homes of Egyptians and the homes of their servants. They climbed all over the people, into their beds, and into their ovens. And when Moses called for the frogs to leave, they all died—"And they gathered them together upon heaps: and the land stank." (Exodus 8:14)

3. Lice

Aaron followed God's command and changed all of the dust in Egypt to massive swarms of lice. "It became lice in man, and in beast; all the dust of the land became lice throughout all the land of Egypt." (Exodus 8:17)

4. Flies

Moses delivered the Lord's Word to the Pharaoh: if he did not free the Israelites, God would send swarms of flies to Egypt. When the Pharaoh refused, the flies arrived. "There came a grievous swarm of flies into the house of Pharaoh, and into his servants' houses, and into all the land of Egypt: the land was corrupted by reason of the swarm of flies." (Exodus 8:24)

5. Livestock

Egyptian livestock were the next target due to the Pharaoh's refusal. All of the Egyptian cattle, horses, donkeys, camels, oxen, and sheep were slaughtered; the livestock of Israelites were left unharmed. (Exodus 9:3-7)

God brought ten plagues upon Egypt because the Pharaoh refused to free the people of Israel from slavery. The plagues were spread over for the Pharaoh to be be obstinate about it (Exodus 5:2), and they showed the power of the Lord both to the Israelites and to the rest of the world (Exodus 9:16-17). The plagues affected all of Egypt, but left the Israelites untouched.

6. Boils

God commanded Moses and Aaron to take ashes from their furnace and sprinkle them toward heaven in front of the Pharaoh. The ashes became dust that rained down upon the Egyptians, becoming boils and sores on their skin and the skin of their animals. (Exodus 9:10)

7. Hail

"I will cause it to rain a very grievous hail, such as hath not been in Egypt since the foundation thereof even until now." (Exodus 9:18) Moses delivered the Lord's Word to the Pharaoh, but still he ignored His warning. The Israelites sheltered their families and livestock while hail and fire thundered down upon the Egyptians, killing those caught under it, and burning their lands and trees.

8. Locusts

The plague of locusts built upon the previous plague of hail and fire. Not only did the locusts arrive, but they ate all of the plants and trees that were spared from the raining hail. The locusts covered every home, inside and out; they crawled upon every man, woman, and child; and they swarmed so densely that the Egyptians could not even see the earth. (Exodus 10:4-6)

9. Darkness

The ninth plague brought darkness over Egypt for three days. The Egyptians could not see each other, and they could not leave their houses. But God again favored the Israelites, and they had light in their homes. (Exodus 10:21-23)

10. Firstborn sons and livestock

The Israelites were spared from the last plague by sacrificing the paschal lamb and marking their doors with the lamb's blood (where the term "Passover" came from). God killed all of the firstborn Egyptian sons and animals. "There was a great cry in Egypt; for there was not a house where there was not one dead." (Exodus 12:30) The Pharaoh relented and released the people of Israel, triggering the Exodus.

START: EGYPT

EXODUS:
ROADMAP TO THE RED SEA

After the Pharaoh agreed to free the Israelites from slavery, God commanded Moses to take them away and escape to Canaan, the Israelites' Promised Land. Moses led his people out of Egypt, but not without the Pharaoh and his armies in pursuit. It was at the Red Sea that God put a stop to their chase: He had Moses part the Red Sea, allowing the Israelites to cross unharmed and escape to safety on the other side. The Egyptians, however, were destroyed in transit.

JERUSALEM

The Israelites took
the bones of Joseph
with them as they
traveled from Egypt
to Succoth.

The Lord traveled with
them as they went,
moving as a pillar of
cloud during the day,
and as a pillar of fire at
night, so as to lead the
way in the darkness.

Next they moved to Etham,
where they camped at the
edge of the wilderness.

SUCCOTH

At the edge of the Red Sea,
per the Lord's instruction,
Moses held his rod and
lifted his hand over the
waters, parting the sea
and allowing the Israelites
to pass to the other side,
safely and on dry land.

As they camped, the
Lord hardened the
Pharaoh's heart, and
had him take his
army to pursue
the Israelites.

The Egyptians pursued, but
in the morning Moses raised
his hand again, closing the
waters down upon them and
destroying the army.

God instructed Moses to
change course, and lead
the people to camp by
the sea, at Pihahiroth.

ETHAM

PIHAHIROTH

**END: THE OTHER SIDE
OF THE RED SEA**
Once they reached the other side,
Moses and the Israelites sang a song
of praise (called "Moses' Song").
Then, later, Miriam (Moses' sister)
offered a briefer, but equally famous,
song of praise for Israel's deliverance
(called "Miriam's Song").

10 FACTS

ABOUT THE 10

COMMANDMENTS

When the people of Israel fled Egypt, Moses led them to the wilderness of Sinai. God called Moses up to the top of Mount Sinai to give him the Ten Commandments, which were written on two stone tablets. God instructed Moses that if his people kept the covenant with Him—and upheld the Ten Commandments—God would favor the Israelites above all people.

I
THOU SHALT HAVE NO OTHER GODS BEFORE ME

II
THOU SHALT MAKE NO FALSE IDOLS

III
THOU SHALT NOT TAKE THE NAME OF THE LORD IN VAIN

IV
REMEMBER TO KEEP THE SABBATH DAY HOLY

V
HONOR YOUR FATHER AND MOTHER

VI
THOU SHALT NOT KILL

VII
THOU SHALT NOT COMMIT ADULTERY

VIII
THOU SHALT NOT STEAL

IX
THOU SHALT NOT BEAR FALSE WITNESS AGAINST YOUR NEIGHBOR

X
THOU SHALT NOT COVET

1 There are two different versions of the Ten Commandments in the Bible! They can be found in Exodus 20 and Deuteronomy 5.

EXODUS 20   DEUTERONOMY 5

4 For centuries, the Ten Commandments were kept inside the Ark of the Covenant.

7 Jews and Christians honor the fourth Commandment, keep the Sabbath day holy, on different days. For Jews, the Sabbath begins Friday night and ends Saturday night. Most Christians observe Sunday as a day of rest.

2

The Ten Commandments fall into two categories: your duties to God and your responsibilities to other people.

3

Another word for the Ten Commandments is the "Decalogue." The *deca-* prefix means "ten," and *logos* is the Greek word for "word." *Decalogue* comes from the Greek word *dekálogos*.

5

The Ten Commandments are not limited to Christianity and Judaism. They also have an important role in the ethical system of Islam.

6

Certain terms in the Ten Commandments offer a wide range of possible interpretation. For example, *covet* can be translated as "conspire against," but the Hebrew language suggests a connotation of "desire."

8

The Ten Commandments are not just a list of rules to follow. Following them should free us from the consequences of sin. Taken this way, they offer us a better life and a more harmonious world.

9

In the Quran, the Ten Commandments are discussed in Surah Al-An'am, 6:151-153, and Surah Al- Isra', 17:23-39.

10

A second set of stones was given to Moses after he broke the first set. You can read the story in Exodus 32:19 and 34:1-4.

CONSTRUCTING THE ARK OF THE COVENANT

The Ark of the Covenant, also called the Ark of the Testimony, was a sacred chest covered in gold that housed the two stone tablets inscribed with the Ten Commandments. The Ark was a physical representation of the covenant God made with the Israelites. It represented God's presence among His people. God gave Moses the designs for the Ark when the Israelites were at Mount Sinai, after they left Egypt. (Exodus 25:10–24)

2 GOLDEN CHERUBIM

were forged and placed at both ends of the mercy seat. The cherubim were a physical representation of a heavenly being. They faced each other, with wings stretched over the seat to cover the Ark.

The Ark was made of shittim wood (probably a kind of acacia wood).

The Ark was overlayed with pure gold—on the inside and out.

The Levites (priests) were charged with the job of carrying the Ark whenever the Israelites were traveling or marching to battle. The Ark was carried 2,000 cubits (3,000 feet) in front of the Israelites. This was for at least two reasons—to show reverence, but also, very practically, so that the Israelites might properly discern the direction in which the Ark was guiding them: "Ye have not passed this way heretofore." (Joshua 3:4)

ARK DIMENSIONS:

2½ cubits (3¾ feet) long
×
1½ cubits (2¼ feet) wide
×
1½ cubits (2¼ feet) high

Moses tasks Bezaleel—assisted by Aholiab—with the job of building the Ark. (Exodus 31) It is noteworthy that Exodus tells us that Bezaleel was filled with the Spirit of God, so as to have the inspiration to fulfill his sacred commission.

God told the Israelites that if they created the Ark to these specifications, He would communicate with them from above the mercy seat, in between the cherubim. (Exodus 25:22)

THE "MERCY SEAT" (LID)
was made of pure gold, and measured
2½ cubits (3¾ feet) long
×
1½ cubits (2¼ feet) wide

The Israelites were instructed to place the stone tablets inscribed with the Ten Commandments into the Ark. (Exodus 25:16)

There were
4 RINGS
placed on the Ark along the corners (2 on each side).

The staves were not to be taken from the Ark!

GILDED STAVES
(poles) made of shittim wood were placed through the rings to carry the vessel.

When carried, the Ark was always covered with blue cloth and with animal skins, to protect it and conceal it from the view of anyone, including the Levites who carried it.

The 7 Sacred Feasts of Israel

In the Hebrew language, the term *feasts* means "the appointed times." The feasts can also be called the "holy convocations." The feasts celebrate historical events in the Old Testament and the agricultural cycles the Israelites experienced, and also offer predictions for events yet to come. The timing and sequence of each sacred feast corresponds to the sacred stories of the Israelites. These are days to reflect upon the interactions between the Lord and mankind.

TRUMPETS (ROSH HASHANA)

Corresponding Old Testament Passages: Leviticus 23:23–25
Hebrew Calendar Date: Tishri 1
Roman Calendar Date: September/October
Meaning: A memorial of blowing trumpets; the stories where Israel conquered.
New Testament Idea: Second Coming of Christ

YOM KIPPUR (ATONEMENT)

Corresponding Old Testament Passages: Leviticus 23:26–32
Hebrew Calendar Date: Tishri 10
Roman Calendar Date: September/October
Meaning: A day of confession; cleansing the Israelites and the temple.
New Testament Idea: Great Judgment

TABERNACLES

Corresponding Old Testament Passages: Leviticus 23:33–34
Hebrew Calendar Date: Tishri 15–22
Roman Calendar Date: September/October
Meaning: To remember that God provided the Israelites shelter in the wilderness in their escape from slavery.
New Testament Idea: New Heaven and New Earth

THE FALL FEASTS

KISLEV

CHESVAN

DEC

NOV

OCT

TISHRI

SEP

AUG

JUL

ELUL

AV

TAMMUZ

THE SPRING FEASTS

TEVET

AV
ADAR
NISAN
IYYAR
SIVAN

JAN
FEB
MAR
APR
MAY
JUN

PASSOVER

Corresponding Old Testament Passages: Exodus 12, Leviticus 23:5
Hebrew Calendar Date: Nisan 14–15
Roman Calendar Date: First full moon of spring
Meaning: The Feast of Salvation. Israel's freedom from slavery. The Israelites were spared from the tenth plague of Egypt by sacrificing a lamb and placing its blood over their doors.
New Testament Idea: The Crucifixion

UNLEAVENED BREAD

Corresponding Old Testament Passages: Leviticus 23:6–8
Hebrew Calendar Date: Nisan 15–22
Roman Calendar Date: March/April
Meaning: In their rush to escape slavery, the Israelites lacked time for bread to rise. Avoid all leavened foods, a symbol of evil.
New Testament Idea: Last Supper

FIRST FRUITS OF THE HARVEST

Corresponding Old Testament Passages: Leviticus 23:9–14
Hebrew Calendar Date: Nisan 16
Roman Calendar Date: March/April
Meaning: Give thanks for the Lord's gifts and the fertility of the land.
New Testament Idea: The Resurrection

PENTECOST

Corresponding Old Testament Passages: Leviticus 23:15–22
Hebrew Calendar Date: Sivan 6–7
Roman Calendar Date: Late May/early June
Meaning: Begins the summer harvest. Two loaves of leavened bread are offered.
New Testament Idea: Church's Birthday (Arrival of the Holy Spirit)

THE 12 SPIES
AND THE 40 YEARS OF BANISHMENT

The story of the twelve spies, as told in NUMBERS 13, centers on ancient tribal rulers of Israel, and their punishment for disobeying the Lord's commands. During the flight from Egypt, Moses charged spies with the task of searching the wilderness for forty days to find a home for the Israelites. (This task reflects Abraham's covenant with God: He had told Abraham his descendants would have a Promised Land in Canaan.) Ten of the twelve spies doubted the Lord's promise, and initially convinced the Israelites that the Promised Land was not hospitable for them to enter. As punishment for their doubt, God banished the Israelites to wander the desert wilderness for forty years.

Some scholars believe the term *spies* actually refers to a Hebrew translation of "princes." It also could be translated to mean "deserters."

THE SPIES

Shammua (tribe of Reuben)

Shaphat (tribe of Simeon)

Caleb (tribe of Judah)

Igal (tribe of Issachar)

Oshea (Joshua) (tribe of Ephraim)

Palti (tribe of Benjamin)

Gaddiel (tribe of Zebulun)

Gaddi (tribe of Manasseh)

Ammiel (tribe of Dan)

Sethur (tribe of Asher)

Nahbi (tribe of Naphtali)

Geuel (tribe of Gad)

JOSHUA AND CALEB

Joshua and Caleb were the only two spies to report the truth about the land: it was possible for the Israelites to conquer the Canaanites and take the land, as God had promised.

- Joshua survived the forty years in the wilderness. Because of his faith and devotion, God deemed him the successor to Moses. Joshua led the Israelites to victory in the wilderness, delivering the Promised Land to them and upholding the covenant with the Lord.

- Caleb also survived the years in the desert. He helped the Israelites defeat their enemies and settle in the Promised Land.

- Joshua and Caleb were the only men of their generation allowed in the Promised Land.

THE OTHER 10 SPIES

The other ten spies initially admitted to Moses that the land was fertile and brought the fruit of the lands: "Surely it floweth with milk and honey." (Numbers 13:27)

They convinced the Israelites that the risk was too dangerous, and that God would not be able to deliver them from their enemies. They described many strong people, great walled cities, and giants inhabiting the lands.

Because the ten spies lied to the Israelites, they were cursed with a plague, and died painful deaths.

THE ENEMIES

The Israelites' foes were many, but God had promised them victory despite the grave challenges of battle. But the ten rebellious spies convinced the Israelites that there were too many enemies to take on. Their enemies included:

- THE CHILDREN OF ANAK (descendants of giants!)
- THE AMALEKITES, who lived south of Jerusalem, near the Great Sea
- THE HITTITES, THE JEBUSITES, AND THE AMORITES, who dwelled in the mountains south of Jerusalem, and east of the Amalekites
- THE CANAANITES, who lived in between the Great Sea (Mediterranean) and the Jordan River

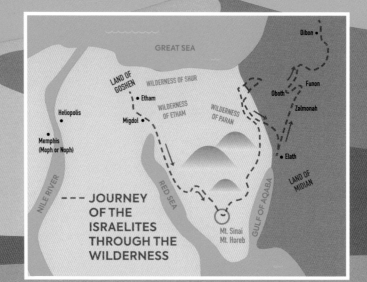

JOURNEY OF THE ISRAELITES THROUGH THE WILDERNESS

Because the Israelites were made to wander in the wilderness for so long, nearly an entire generation of men perished in the sand.

7 STEPS TO THE
Destruction of Jericho

The walled city of Jericho was a stronghold in Canaan, a land the Lord had promised to Abraham and all of his descendants. Since Noah had cursed Canaan to slavery, the lands of Canaan were to go to the Israelites, but they were taken into slavery by the Egyptians. When Moses freed them, he ordered the Israelites to seize all of Canaan, starting with the first city, Jericho. Under Joshua's command, the priests and people of Israel demolished the city and annihilated its people. (Joshua 6)

4

3

2

1

6

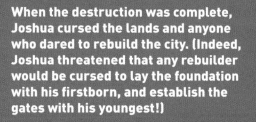

When the destruction was complete, Joshua cursed the lands and anyone who dared to rebuild the city. (Indeed, Joshua threatened that any rebuilder would be cursed to lay the foundation with his firstborn, and establish the gates with his youngest!)

5

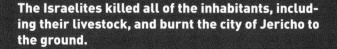

Amidst the attack, only Rahab and her family were saved from death and destruction, because they had sheltered Joshua's spies. Joshua's spies rescued them from Jericho.

The Israelites killed all of the inhabitants, including their livestock, and burnt the city of Jericho to the ground.

All of the silver, gold, brass, and iron were saved from the city, and they were placed within the house of the Lord—consecrated now to the Lord.

After the last march on the seventh day, the Israelite priests took up the Ark of the Covenant, and blasted their trumpets toward the city. Obeying God's command, all of the Israelite people shouted and screamed at the city walls, causing them to fall flat.

The Lord commanded Joshua to lead the Israelite soldiers and priests in marches around the city walls. They were to march around the city once a day for six days, carrying the Ark of the Covenant. Seven priests would carry seven trumpets made of rams' horns. On the seventh day, the Israelites were ordered to march around the city seven times.

Joshua sent spies into the city of Jericho, to get an understanding of the land and determine the mood of the people. Joshua's messengers were hidden in Rahab the harlot's home with her family. The spies learned that the people of Jericho were in fear of the Israelites—prompting them to attack.

MAPPING THE
CONQUEST
of CANAAN

The **BOOK OF JOSHUA** transitions from Moses as its protagonist to Joshua. After Moses' death, God orders Joshua to conquer Canaan, the Promised Land. Chapters 2–11 focus on this massive campaign. The success of the Israelites' conquest reflects the Lord's message to His chosen ones: if they have faith, God keeps His promise to protect them, despite the dangers of battle.

FOLLOW THE CONQUEST

The map highlights Joshua and the Israelites' path to reclaiming the Promised Land, as stated in the Book of Joshua, starting with their arrival in Jericho.

1. **The River Jordan:** Joshua leads the Israelites across the river (3:6–17)
2. **Gilgal:** The Israelites make camp (4:19)
3. **Jericho:** The Israelites take the city and enter Canaan (6:1–27)
4. **Ai:** The Israelites ambush the city (8:1–29)
5. **The Amorites:** The Israelites attack, as they did in Ai (9–10:10)
6. **Valley of Ajalon:** Joshua chases the Amorites through the valley (10:9–14)
7. **Makkedah:** Joshua traps the kings and destroys the city (10:16–28)
8. **Libnah:** The Israelites fight the city (10:29–30)
9. **Lachish:** They ambush the city and smite the king (10:31–33)
10. **Eglon:** The Israelites fight and the city falls (10:34–35)
11. **Hebron:** They take this city as well (10:36–37)
12. **Debir:** The Israelites surround and conquer (10:38–39)
13. **Kadeshbarnea:** Joshua smites them all (10:41)
14. **Gaza:** The Israelites storm northward and conquer (10:1)
15. **Waters of Merom:** Sneak attack on the northern coalition (11:5–7)
16. **Zidon:** Hot on their heels as the enemy retreats (11:8)
17. **The Valley of Mizpeh:** Israel marches in pursuit (11:8)
18. **Hazor:** Joshua moves to take Hazor (11:10)

16 17
15 18

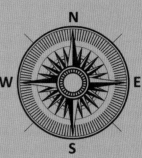

N

W E

S

5 4
6 3 2 1
7
8
9
10 11
14 12
13

After the conquest was complete, Joshua divided the land among the twelve tribes, with each tribe receiving the following number of towns:

9 towns for Simeon and Judah

4 towns each for Benjamin, Ephraim, Dan, Manasseh, Issachar, Asher, Zebulun, Reuben, and Gad

3 towns for Naphtali

THE 12 JUDGES OF ISRAEL

1

OTHNIEL delivered the Israelites from eight years of oppression under Cushan-rishathaim, the king of Aram-Naharaim in Mesopotamia, after the Lord sold them because of their idolatry and sins. He brought peace to the people for forty years.

2

EHUD was a left-handed Judge who saved the Israelites from Moabite rule by stabbing the king of Moab, Eglon, in the stomach.

3

SHAMGAR fought off Philistine invaders, and killed 600 of them with an ox goad (a spur to guide livestock).

7

JAIR ruled for twenty-two years. The number thirty is important to his story: Jair had thirty sons who rode on thirty ass colts, and together they held thirty cities.

8

JEPHTHAH led the Israelites in a battle to defeat the Ammonites. As a thanks to God, he vowed to sacrifice the first thing that exited his home. Sadly, when he returned to his house, his daughter came forth to greet him—and he only then realized the enormous tragedy of his being bound to such a vow. Jephthah is also central to the story of the "Shibboleth." Those who pronounced the name wrong (when they were asked to say it) revealed themselves to be Ephraimites—and hence, enemies of Israel.

9

IBZAN was another Judge without much background. Thirty is another important number here: he had thirty sons, and thirty daughters, whom he sent abroad. He took in thirty daughters-in-law for his thirty sons!

THE BOOK OF JUDGES is set in a dark period of ancient Israel's history. It weaves together many stories about twelve leaders of Israel, who were called the Judges. They were legal rulers and counselors, as well as military and political figures. The book explains how the Israelites rebelled against the Lord, and continually had to ask for His forgiveness and salvation. Despite their idolatry, disobedience, and sins, God always found a way to forgive those who repented and to save the Israelites from their enemies. The Book of Judges is an excellent example of the Lord's devotion to the covenant He made with Abraham.

4

DEBORAH was the only female Judge. Deborah was a prophet who predicted the Israelites would lead an attack against Jabin, the king of Canaan, and his more famous general, Sisera, who had been oppressing the Israelites.

5

GIDEON's triumph was truly an underdog story. He led just 300 men to victory against a large army of the Midianites in a daring nighttime attack of their camp. He is commemorated by the name of the group famous for distributing the Bibles found in many hotel rooms.

6

TOLA is perhaps the least remembered Judge. Neither his life nor the feats he performed for the Israelites are detailed, only that he ruled for twenty-three years.

10

ELON was a a Zebulonite who judged Israel for ten years. He was buried in Aijalon (a city in Zebulun).

11

ABDON was the son of Hillel, from a place called Pirathon (site unknown). He judged Israel for eight years. He is presumed to have been wealthy: he had forty sons and thirty nephews, and gave all of them donkeys to ride.

12

SAMSON may be the most popular Judge of all. Given immense powers of strength, he was famous for killing a lion, destroying an entire army by himself, and pulling down a temple with his bare hands. A Nazirite, he vowed to abstain from alcohol, and never to cut his hair or to shave. Samson fell in love with Delilah, to whom he confided the secret of his strength—his long (uncut) hair.

ALL ABOUT RUTH

> **"** Intreat me not to leave thee...for whither thou goest, I will go; and where thou lodgest, I will lodge: thy people shall be my people, and thy God my God.**"**
>
> (RUTH 1:16)

Lessons to Remember

→ Though Ruth was from Moab, she accepted the Israelite people as her own and more importantly, THEIR GOD AS HER GOD.

→ SUPPORTING YOUR FAMILY (like Ruth and Naomi did in the face of famine and death) can lead you to safety and salvation.

→ ALL PEOPLE ARE IMPORTANT TO GOD. Even though Ruth was not an Israelite, she still was an important person in God's plan: she is a crucial figure in the genealogy of Jesus.

The Book of Ruth details the beautiful story of Ruth, a Moabitess (Moab was an ancient kingdom east of Israel). She forged a special bond with her mother-in-law, Naomi. Although Ruth was not born an Israelite, she accepted the Hebrews as her own people, and worshipped God as the one true Lord. Together Ruth and Naomi faced adversity, and in their faith and support for one another, they thrived in Bethlehem. Ruth's story is one of second chances, and one that speaks to God's plan for all people.

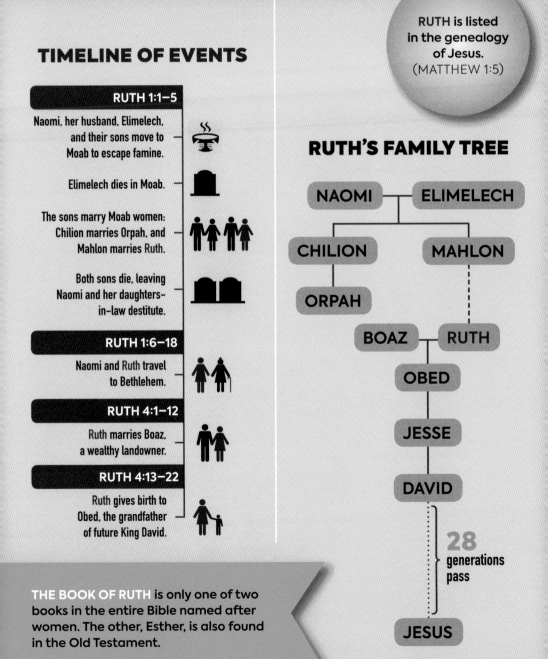

TIMELINE OF EVENTS

RUTH is listed in the genealogy of Jesus. (MATTHEW 1:5)

RUTH 1:1–5

Naomi, her husband, Elimelech, and their sons move to Moab to escape famine.

Elimelech dies in Moab.

The sons marry Moab women: Chilion marries Orpah, and Mahlon marries Ruth.

Both sons die, leaving Naomi and her daughters-in-law destitute.

RUTH 1:6–18

Naomi and Ruth travel to Bethlehem.

RUTH 4:1–12

Ruth marries Boaz, a wealthy landowner.

RUTH 4:13–22

Ruth gives birth to Obed, the grandfather of future King David.

RUTH'S FAMILY TREE

NAOMI — ELIMELECH

CHILION — MAHLON

ORPAH

BOAZ — RUTH

OBED

JESSE

DAVID

28 generations pass

JESUS

THE BOOK OF RUTH is only one of two books in the entire Bible named after women. The other, Esther, is also found in the Old Testament.

DAVID AND GOLIATH:

A HERO'S TALE BY THE NUMBERS

1 SAMUEL 17 tells the story of David and Goliath, which in modern times is synonymous with underdog tales. King Saul and the Israelites were battling the Philistines, and were faced with enslavement if they were to lose the war. Goliath, a giant Philistine warrior, challenged the Israelites as the armies camped at opposite ends of the Valley of Elah. King Saul called upon the small and humble David to face Goliath, and this unlikely hero defeated the menacing soldier with his slingshot and his faith in the Lord.

David's father, Jesse, the Bethlehemite, had

8 SONS

David was his **8th**, or youngest, son.

Jesse's **3 ELDEST SONS** ELIAB, ABINADAB, and SHAMMAH, went to fight for King Saul in the Israelite army.

While the 3 eldest were away at war, Jesse instructed David to bring food to his brothers and their leaders. He brought:

1 EPHAH (about ⅔ bushel) **OF DRIED CORN**

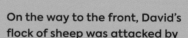

10 LOAVES OF BREAD

10 WHEELS OF CHEESE

On the way to the front, David's flock of sheep was attacked by

2 PREDATORS,
1 bear and 1 lion.

With God's help, David slew them both.

For **40** days,
Goliath mocked and challenged the Israelites, taunting them into battle.

When he encountered Goliath, David was armed with just

1 slingshot
and **5** smooth stones.

1 **HIT**
was all it took for David to knock down Goliath. David grabbed Goliath's sword and cut off his head; the Philistines fled in terror.

Goliath was a massive man to behold. He is described as:

Standing
6 **CUBITS TALL**
(9 FEET)

Wearing
4 PIECES of BRASS:
1 HELMET
2 GREAVES (shin guards)
1 CHEST PLATE

Wearing
1 COAT OF MAIL
weighing
5,000 SHEKELS
(more than 155 pounds)

Protected by
1 GUARD
carrying
1 SHIELD
in front of him

Carrying
1 IRON SPEAR
its head weighing
600 SHEKELS
(nearly 19 pounds)

KING SAUL'S CAMPAIGN

1 SAMUEL details an ancient feud between Saul, the first king of Israel, and David, the warrior. The feud began after a battle with the Philistines. Women from the cities credited David with killing ten thousands—but Saul only thousands (1 Samuel 18:6–7). Saul became jealous of David's success and praise, and this envy and hatred consumed his life. Despite perilous situations and several assassination attempts on David's life, God continually protected David, according to His covenant with Israel. Saul's actions reflect his fall from grace in the Lord's eyes, a precursor to David becoming a great king of Israel.

DAVID AVOIDS SAUL'S JAVELIN

1 Samuel 18:10–11

As the jealousy set in, Saul threw a javelin at David, attempting to pin him to a wall, but David was able to avoid it.

JONATHAN WARNS DAVID

1 Samuel 19:1–6

Saul told his servants and his son Jonathan that David should be killed on sight. But Jonathan loved David, and warned him of the plan, so David hid until Jonathan talked his father out of the murder plot.

GOD PROTECTS DAVID

1 Samuel 19:20–24

Saul and his messengers continued to pursue David. This time, the Spirit of God came to David to protect him, and hid him from his attackers.

AGAINST DAVID

DAVID AVOIDS SAUL'S SECOND JAVELIN

1 Samuel 19:9–10

Saul attempted to kill David a second time with a spear. He threw the javelin into the wall, but David "slipped away out of Saul's presence," and fled for his life.

DAVID ESCAPES THROUGH A WINDOW

1 Samuel 19:11–18

The morning after the second javelin was thrown, Saul sent assassins to David's house to kill him. Michal, David's wife, warned him of the danger, and helped him escape out of a window. Michal placed a decoy in the bed to distract the assassins and deceive Saul.

SALVATION IN THE WILDERNESS

1 Samuel 23:14

While traveling in the wilderness of Ziph, Saul pursued David every day. David hid himself on a mountain, and the Lord prevented Saul from finding him.

THE RISE OF KING DAVID

The narratives in **1** and **2 SAMUEL** discuss the ascent of Israel's first kings, Saul and David, and how the Lord chose David over Saul to continue His line, a dynasty that would create the line of successors to Jesus.

2 Samuel 7:18–29

2 Samuel 7:1–17

1 Samuel 16:1–13

1 Samuel 15:3–26

1 Samuel 9:15–17

A CURSED HOUSE

Chapters 11–21 in 2 Samuel discuss a time when David disobeyed God's instruction. He committed adultery with Bathsheba, and then plotted to kill her husband. As a result, the Lord cursed his house; for the remainder of his time as king, there were problems within his family.

The Lord chose David's house as the ruler of the Israelites. The verses state that God will be David's father, and David will be His son. This mirrors the coming of Jesus out of David's lineage: He who would become the Son of God and lead the Israelites to salvation.

The Lord chose David over Saul to continue the covenant He made with Abraham. He pledged an eternal covenant with the house of David, ensuring the longevity of David's dynasty.

God rejected Saul and chose David to be the new king of Israel.

God ordered Saul to destroy the nation of Amalek—every person and animal. Saul annihilated the people, but kept the best animals to sacrifice to God. Samuel informed Saul that by disobeying, Saul was no longer the favored king of Israel.

The Israelites asked God for a new king. The Lord chose Samuel to bless Saul as the first king of Israel.

KING SOLOMON:

WISE BUT FLAWED

Solomon's name is synonymous with wisdom. Hailed as one of the richest and wisest kings of Israel, this son of David also made mistakes. Although he was a king and an important figure in the line of David, his flaws highlight the important fact that he was still human, and needed to yield to the will and power of God. Here, some of his most notable triumphs, and biggest mistakes, are discussed.

GOOD DECISIONS

The following are examples of how Solomon's knowledge and reason prevailed in the face of adversity.

Turning to God

The Lord appeared to Solomon in a dream and said he could ask for anything. Solomon asked for **"an understanding heart to…discern between good and bad."** (1 KINGS 3:9) This pleased the Lord, and He gave Solomon a **"wise and an understanding heart; so that there was none like thee before thee."** (1 KINGS 3:12)

The Baby Debacle

In 1 Kings 3, two harlots approached Solomon: both women gave birth to sons, but one son died. The woman who lost her child took the other for her own. Solomon called for a sword to cut the baby—each mother could have half. The true mother cried out to save her baby, even if it meant giving him up. Solomon knew the true mother, and returned the baby to her.

> So king Solomon exceeded all the kings of the earth for riches and for wisdom. And all the earth sought to Solomon, to hear his wisdom, which God had put in his heart."
>
> (1 KINGS 10:23–24)

BAD DECISIONS

Though Solomon was celebrated for his wisdom, ultimately, he made mistakes too. As a mortal, he was flawed by his sins and transgressions.

Turning His Back to God

Solomon's foreign wives **"turned away his heart"** from God. (1 KINGS 11:3) The Lord warned Solomon to cease his idolatry. Solomon ignored Him, and God delivered punishment: He would take Solomon's kingdom and give it to his servant when Solomon's son was reigning. (1 KINGS 11:9–12) This led to the kingdom's separation: Israel in the north and Judah in the south.

Marriage to Outsiders

"Solomon loved many strange women, together with the daughter of Pharaoh, women of the Moabites, Ammonites, Edomites, Zidonians, and Hittites." (1 KINGS 11:1) And he loved *many* women, indeed: he had 700 wives and 300 concubines!

Idolatry

The Lord warned Solomon that if he married so many foreign women, they would turn him away to worship their own gods. But Solomon could not resist them, and the sins that God predicted would happen came true. (1 KINGS 11:2)

> And the Lord was angry with Solomon, because his heart was turned from the Lord God of Israel."
>
> (1 KINGS 11:9)

GOD VERSUS BAAL:
Elijah's Battle for the True Lord

In **1 Kings 18,** Elijah confronts King Ahab and his followers of Israel who had been worshipping Baal, an ancient Canaanite and Phoenician god. Elijah gathers Ahab, the prophets of Baal, other idolaters who worship a god named Asherah, and the people of Israel at Mount Carmel to confront them with their sin. Elijah puts Baal to the test to prove to his followers who the true Lord is, and so the Israelites can atone for their idolatry

THE SETTING

Israel had been experiencing a drought brought on by the people's idol worship.

THE SHOWDOWN

450 Baal prophets + 400 Asherah prophets vs. Elijah.

THE CHALLENGE

Burn a bull on an altar without lighting a fire.

THE PROPHETS

The prophets of Baal cried out to their god to light the fire, but no fire was lit. They continued to cry out and slash themselves with knives, but their pleas went unanswered.

ELIJAH

Elijah had the Israelites douse the sacrifice and altar with water. Elijah prayed to God, who set the sacrifice on fire and evaporated the water.

THE VICTOR

The people of Israel repented, turned their hearts toward the Lord, and declared Him the true God.

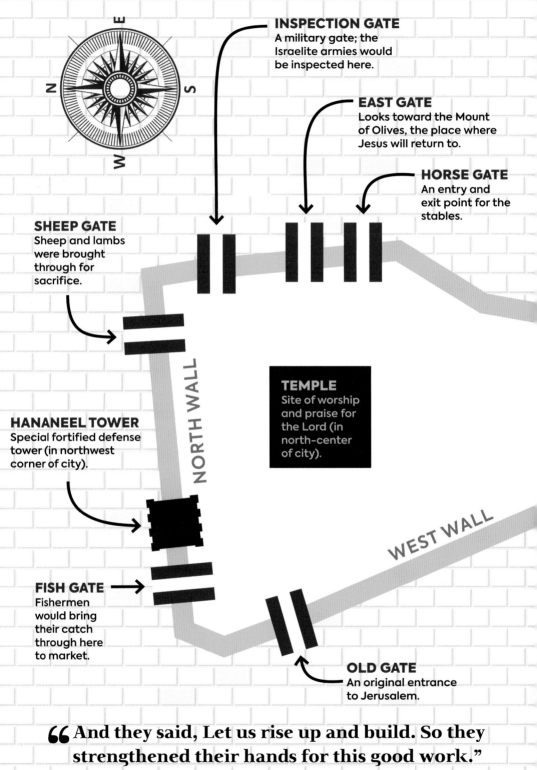

INSPECTION GATE
A military gate; the Israelite armies would be inspected here.

EAST GATE
Looks toward the Mount of Olives, the place where Jesus will return to.

HORSE GATE
An entry and exit point for the stables.

SHEEP GATE
Sheep and lambs were brought through for sacrifice.

HANANEEL TOWER
Special fortified defense tower (in northwest corner of city).

TEMPLE
Site of worship and praise for the Lord (in north-center of city).

NORTH WALL

WEST WALL

FISH GATE
Fishermen would bring their catch through here to market.

OLD GATE
An original entrance to Jerusalem.

66 **And they said, Let us rise up and build. So they strengthened their hands for this good work.”**
(NEHEMIAH 2:18)

NEHEMIAH:
BUILDING THE WALLS OF JERUSALEM

Nehemiah was a servant to the king of Persia when the Israelites were returning to a crumbling Jerusalem after years of captivity by the Babylonians. Nehemiah traveled to his homeland as a new governor, and led the Israelites to rebuild the walls. The walls were a physical barrier to protect the Israelites from enemies, but they also had a greater meaning: they represented the Israelites rebuilding their faith in God, and revealed how God once again showed favor upon them.

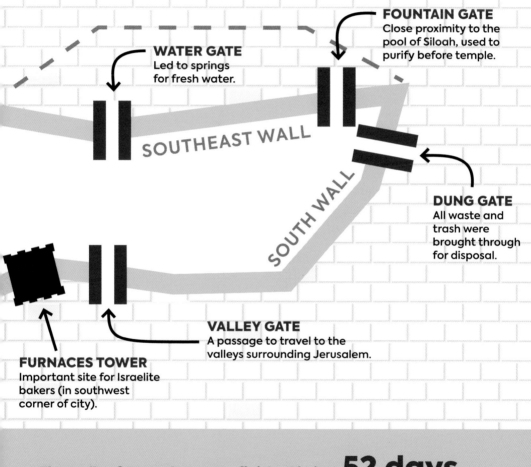

FOUNTAIN GATE
Close proximity to the pool of Siloah, used to purify before temple.

WATER GATE
Led to springs for fresh water.

SOUTHEAST WALL

SOUTH WALL

DUNG GATE
All waste and trash were brought through for disposal.

VALLEY GATE
A passage to travel to the valleys surrounding Jerusalem.

FURNACES TOWER
Important site for Israelite bakers (in southwest corner of city).

>> The walls of Jerusalem were finished in just **52 days.**

>> By the **7th** month, all of the children of Israel were in their city.
(NEHEMIAH 7:73)

>> Nehemiah ruled for **12 years** as governor of Jerusalem, and worked to rebuild the Jewish community.

ESTHER:
STAR OF THE PERSIAN EMPIRE

The **BOOK OF ESTHER** tells the story of a young orphaned Jewish woman who was chosen to become the queen of the Persian Empire. Faced with the imminent destruction of her people, Esther risked her life to save her Jewish brothers and sisters, a feat now remembered in the feast of Purim. Important highlights from Esther's extraordinary life are detailed here.

Esther also went by the name Hadassah. *ESTHER* MEANS "STAR" in Persian. Esther was described as "fair and beautiful." (ESTHER 2:7)

" So will I go in unto the king . . . and if I perish, I perish."

(ESTHER 4:16)

Esther was ORPHANED as a young girl. Her older cousin, Mordecai, took her in and raised her as his own daughter.

Esther was chosen among hundreds of other young virgins to be the new QUEEN OF THE PERSIAN EMPIRE. Hotheaded King Ahasuerus divorced his wife, Queen Vashti, after she refused to attend a banquet and publicly scorned her husband.

PURIM, the Jewish holy holiday, is celebrated each year to commemorate the Israelites' deliverance as told in the Book of Esther.

- Haman, the king's vizier, despised Mordecai after Mordecai refused to bow to him. Upon learning Mordecai was Jewish, Haman planned to have him—and all Jews—killed.

- Esther risked her life and asked the king to spare her people. Reminded how Mordecai once foiled an assassination plot against him, King Ahasuerus agreed to save Mordecai and Esther's people.

- The king ordered the Jews to attack their enemies, including Haman and his sons. The resulting battles claimed the lives of 75,000 Persians.

SHUSHAN

The Persian Empire

King Ahasuerus reigned over 127 provinces, from India to Ethiopia. The palace was located in the city of Shushan.

JOB: SUFFERING AND RENEWED FAITH

"This man was the greatest of all the men of the east."
(JOB 1:3)

TESTING GOD, TESTING JOB

Satan came to test the Lord. God boasted about Job's goodness, and Satan said Job would turn if God punished him.

TEST #1

All Job's livestock were stolen or killed.

All his servants were killed.

All of Job's children were killed.

TEST #2

Satan plagued Job with boils from head to toe.

RESULT

Job's wife told him to curse the Lord, but he still refused. Job fell into despair, cursed the day he was born, but kept his faith in the Lord.

Job was a man described as "perfect and upright, and one that feared God, and eschewed evil." (JOB 1:1) Satan wanted to test Job's unwavering faithfulness and God accepted the challenge, with the crucial provision that Satan was not to set his hand upon Job himself. As part of the challenge, Job lost his estate, his health, and everyone he loved, but his trust in God's divine goodness never wavered. God rewarded Job's faith by restoring his health, blessing him with a new family, and doubling his possessions.

RESULT

Job shaved his head in his grief, but did not sin or curse the Lord. Instead, he blessed Him. (JOB 20–21)

BY THE NUMBERS

By acknowledging God's almighty power and the limitations of his own mortality, Job showed his faithfulness. The boils disappeared, Job was blessed with new children, and his estate doubled in size.

BEFORE THE TESTS, JOB HAD:

7 sons **3** daughters

7,000 sheep

3,000 camels

500 oxen

500 asses

AFTER THE TESTS, JOB HAD:

7 sons **3** daughters

14,000 sheep

6,000 camels

1,000 oxen

1,000 asses

THE Authorship OF THE Psalms

The psalms are sacred songs, hymns, and prayers that offer praise to the Lord. The Book of Psalms is composed of 150 songs and prayers. Many of the psalms are ascribed to King David. Scholars believe it is likely that the psalm book as a whole was redacted (or edited to roughly its present format) during the period of the "second temple"—following the period of the Babylonian captivity (539 B.C.). This psalm book of Israel offers you meaningful ways to interpret the Word of God, and can help you gain a deeper appreciation of the Lord and His works.

5 Sections of the Book of Psalms

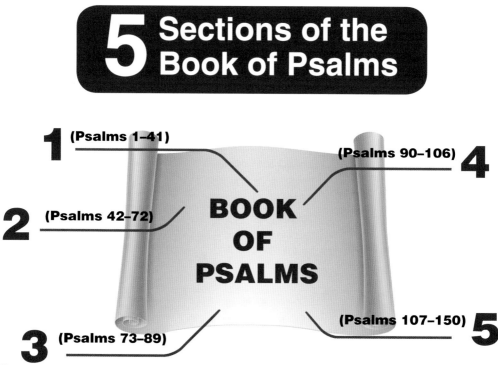

1 (Psalms 1–41)

2 (Psalms 42–72)

3 (Psalms 73–89)

4 (Psalms 90–106)

5 (Psalms 107–150)

BOOK OF PSALMS

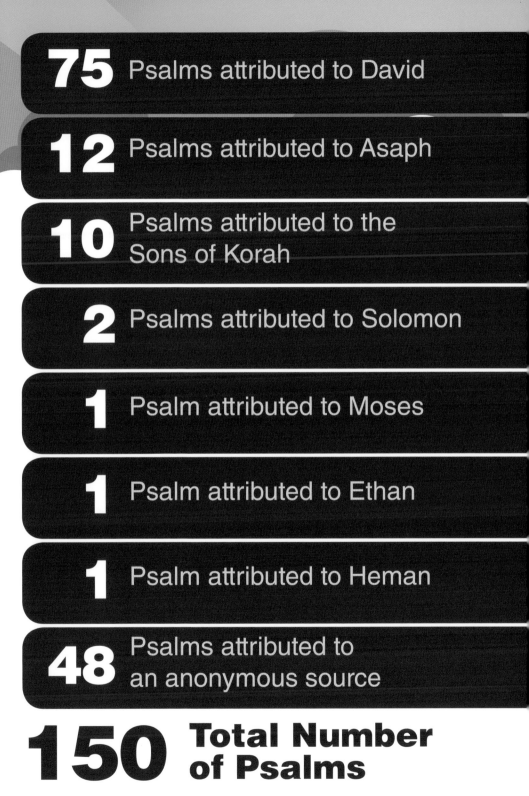

75 Psalms attributed to David

12 Psalms attributed to Asaph

10 Psalms attributed to the Sons of Korah

2 Psalms attributed to Solomon

1 Psalm attributed to Moses

1 Psalm attributed to Ethan

1 Psalm attributed to Heman

48 Psalms attributed to an anonymous source

150 **Total Number of Psalms**

Seeking Wisdom
THROUGH THE *Proverbs*

The **BOOK OF PROVERBS** seeks to offer wisdom and deliver profound messages in simple terms. Indeed, Proverbs 9:10 states, "The fear of the Lord is the beginning of wisdom: and the knowledge of the holy is understanding." The proverbs presented here can be a starting point for your own journey to wisdom through God's Word.

VALUES

The Book of Proverbs often runs counter to the norms, patterns, and value systems of the world around us.

A good name is rather to be chosen than great riches, and loving favour rather than silver and gold. (PROVERBS 22:1)

Devise not evil against thy neighbour, seeing he dwelleth securely by thee. (PROVERBS 3:29)

Open thy mouth, judge righteously, and plead the cause of the poor and needy. (PROVERBS 31:9)

THE MEANING OF LIFE

Implicit in the proverbs' pithy sayings is an understanding of the meaning of life. Our value and worth are connected to our trusting relationship with God, or our obedience to God's precepts.

Trust in the Lord with all thine heart; and lean not unto thine own understanding. (PROVERBS 3:5)

This is a central theme of the Book of Proverbs, and echoes of it are found throughout the book.

MORALITY

Proverbs frequently offers stark contrasts between the ways of evil and good.

The righteousness of the perfect shall direct his way: but the wicked shall fall by his own wickedness. (PROVERBS 11:5)

Where there is no vision, the people perish: but he that keepeth the law, happy is he. (PROVERBS 29:18)

Better is the poor that walketh in his uprightness, than he that is perverse in his ways, though he be rich. (PROVERBS 28:6)

VIRTUOUS BEHAVIOR

The Book of Proverbs is practical in its advice for daily living.

Rob not the poor, because he is poor: neither oppress the afflicted in the gate: For the Lord will plead their cause, and spoil the soul of those that spoiled them. (PROVERBS 22:22-23)

Proverbs makes a priority of teaching simple justice.

The wise shall inherit glory: but shame shall be the promotion of fools. (PROVERBS 3:35)

A gracious woman retaineth honour: and strong men retain riches. (PROVERBS 11:16)

Keep thy heart with all diligence; for out of it are the issues of life. (PROVERBS 4:23)

The fear of the Lord is the beginning of wisdom. (PROVERBS 9:10)

It is understood that "fear" here does not mean "cowering" fear, but "awe" and "reverence."

Death and life are in the power of the tongue: and they that love it shall eat the fruit thereof. (PROVERBS 18:21)

The fear of the Lord is a fountain of life, to depart from the snares of death. (PROVERBS 14:27)

ISAIAH'S
PROPHECIES

BY THE
NUMBERS

130
There are nearly 130 messianic prophecies in the Book of Isaiah.

66
Number of chapters in the Book of Isaiah, the longest prophetic book.

60
Estimated number of years Isaiah preached to the Israelites.

39
After Chapter 39, Isaiah's name is no longer used in the text. (This may speak to the idea that he was not the only author of the book.)

8
Isaiah was an eighth-century B.C. prophet, making his writings nearly 2,800 years old.

1
Isaiah 44:6 presents a clear message of monotheism to the Israelites: "I am the first, and I am the last; and beside me there is no God."

THE
COMING
OF THE
MESSIAH

THE FATE OF THE
ISRAELITES

APPROACHING
"THE DAY OF
THE LORD"

Isaiah is one of the most famous biblical prophets. The sixty-six chapters in his book are filled with predictions that center upon the coming of the Messiah, Jesus Christ. Isaiah also foresaw the fate of the Israelites and, according to Christian tradition, what would happen during the Second Coming of Christ. Some Christians have accordingly called Isaiah the "fifth gospel" because Isaiah speaks about the Messiah profusely. Here, some of the most profound prophecies are discussed.

PROPHECIES

REALIZATIONS

The Messiah will make the ultimate sacrifice for us, and take our sins upon Himself.
(ISAIAH 53:4–5, 7–8)

"For when we were yet without strength, in due time Christ died for the ungodly…while we were yet sinners, Christ died for us."
(ROMANS 5:6–8)

The Lord will choose the Israelites to be His servants, His only people.
(ISAIAH 41:8–9)

"Thou art my servant, O Israel, in whom I will be glorified."
(ISAIAH 49:3)

The Messiah will return (also known as the Second Coming). A great trumpet will sound.
(ISAIAH 27:12–13)

"And the seventh angel sounded; and there were great voices in heaven, saying, The kingdoms of this world are become the kingdoms of our Lord, and of his Christ; and he shall reign for ever and ever."
(REVELATION 11:15)

THE BOOK OF
LAMENTATIONS

The BOOK OF LAMENTATIONS contains five poems (chapters), all describing the city of Jerusalem in different ways.

Through brooding language and dire tones, the book expresses extreme suffering and unheard cries for redemption. All are prayerful and often plaintive cries to God (rather than oracles from God).

CHAPTER 2 highlights the Israelites' sins.

"The Lord was as an enemy: he hath swallowed up Israel, he hath swallowed up all her palaces: he hath destroyed his strong holds, and hath increased in the daughter of Judah mourning and lamentation."

LAMENTATIONS 2:5

CHAPTER 3 speaks of hope through punishment.

"Out of the mouth of the most High proceedeth not evil and good? Wherefore doth a living man complain, a man for the punishment of his sins? Let us search and try our ways, and turn again to the Lord. Let us lift up our heart with our hands unto God in the heavens."

LAMENTATIONS 3:38–41

"How doth the city sit solitary, that was full of people! how is she become as a widow! she that was great among the nations, and princess among the provinces, how is she become tributary! She weepeth sore in the night, and her tears are on her cheeks."

LAMENTATIONS 1:1–2

CHAPTER 4 describes the desolate city.

"The Lord hath accomplished his fury; he hath poured out his fierce anger, and hath kindled a fire in Zion, and it hath devoured the foundations thereof. The kings of the earth, and all the inhabitants of the world, would not have believed that the adversary and the enemy should have entered into the gates of Jerusalem."

LAMENTATIONS 4:11–12

CHAPTER 5 is a prayer for deliverance.

"Thou, O Lord, remainest for ever; thy throne from generation to generation. Wherefore dost thou forget us for ever, and forsake us so long time? Turn thou us unto thee, O Lord, and we shall be turned; renew our days as of old."

LAMENTATIONS 5:19–21

DANIEL, *the* LIONS' DEN, *and* DELIVERANCE

DANIEL 6 tells the famous Old Testament story "Daniel in the Lions' Den," a tale of conspiracy, attempted murder, and redemption. Daniel was the favored first advisor ("president") to King Darius, a role coveted by the other governors ("princes") and advisors serving him. Jealous of his prestige, and unable to find fault in his role, the council conspired against him, and had him thrown into a den of lions. Daniel's faith brought him God's favor. For his enemies, it brought swift justice.

CAUSE

EFFECT

CAUSE	EFFECT
As the ruler of Babylon, King Darius wanted to ensure his power.	The king appointed 120 satraps, or governors, and three advisors, including Daniel, who oversaw the satraps.
Daniel rose to prominence as the king's most trusted advisor.	The satraps and advisors grew jealous of Daniel.
The others forced the king to issue a decree forbidding people to pray to anyone but the king.	Daniel continued to pray to God and was thrown into a lions' den as punishment.
Expecting the lions to attack, Daniel prayed to God.	God sent an angel to the den to keep the lions' mouths closed and save Daniel.
King Darius realized he made a mistake and went to find Daniel in the den.	Daniel was rescued from the den and the others and their families were fed to the lions.
Daniel's faith saved him from the lions' den.	King Darius issued a new decree stating all

ISRAEL'S FALL

CHAPTERS 4–14 OF HOSEA discuss Israel's fall from grace back into sin, most notably by allowing elements of Canaanite religion into its worship. The prophecies in these chapters urge the Israelites to return to their true God, and repent of their sins against Him.

Swearing
(4:2)

Hatred
(9:7–8)

Wickedness
(7:2)

ISRAEL'S SINS

Broken the covenant
(6:7)

Broken judgement
(5:11)

Pride
(5:5)

Alcoholism
(4:11)

FROM GRACE

Lying
(4:2)

Killing
(4:2)

Stealing
(4:2)

"Hear the word of
the Lord, ye children of
Israel: for the Lord hath
a controversy with the
inhabitants of the land,
because there is no truth,
nor mercy, nor knowledge
of God in the land."
(HOSEA 4:1)

Adultery
(4:2)

Rejecting
God's law
(4:6)

Priests
enjoy sins
(4:8)

Prostitution
(4:10–14)

JONAH
AND THE
BIG
FISH
THAT SAVED HIM

THE BOOK OF JONAH tells the story of Jonah, his relationship with God, and the consequences of not following the Lord's wishes. Woven throughout the text are lessons about God's love and mercy, loving your enemies, and making sacrifices for the greater good. By following Jonah's story, you too can learn the significance of honoring the Lord's teachings, and broaden your own understanding of the importance of

One day, God called down to Jonah and told him to preach to the people of Nineveh; the people were wicked and needed to repent. Jonah hated this idea, because the people of Nineveh were the sworn enemies of Israel!

 Jonah fled to the sea to escape the task God charged him with. While on a boat to Tarshish, God sent a mighty tempest to destroy the ship.

 The sailors blamed Jonah for the storm, and cast him overboard to save themselves. The storm ceased as Jonah hit the water.

 God sent a big fish (some call it a whale) to swallow Jonah and save him from drowning. For three days Jonah prayed, repented, and praised the Lord in the belly of the fish.

 God had the fish throw Jonah up on the shores on Nineveh, where he preached to them to repent. The people asked forgiveness for their sins, and God granted them mercy.

 Jonah was angry with God for not destroying his enemies! Jonah sat, seething at the edge of the city, but God created a gourd to shade him from the sun.

 Then God created a worm to eat the gourd, and Jonah wished for death as he withered under the sun. God explained to Jonah that it was just as important to save Jonah's life as it was to save the 120,000 Ninevites (and their cattle!).

Lessons Learned

→ **RESPECT THE LORD,** follow His guidance, and obey His wishes.

→ **LOVE YOUR ENEMY** despite your pride—all life is precious, and even sinners deserve the chance to repent.

→ **IT'S NOT ALWAYS *ALL ABOUT YOU*.** Broaden your horizons and look to the lives of all; strive to aid others and work for the common good.

ZECHARIAH'S 8 VISIONS

The **BOOK OF ZECHARIAH** contains eight visions that offer promises of forgiveness for Israel, blessings of restoration of the land and people from exile, and judgment on the nations that come against God's eternal plans and promises.

1 A Man and Horses Among the Myrtle Trees (ZECHARIAH 1:8-17)

A man rides a red horse into a grove of myrtle trees. Red, speckled, and white horses race out across the world, and find it at peace. Israel was in exile after being spoiled by nations that did not worship God. Although God was angry, He would rebuild His house, forgive their sins, and reestablish the covenant.

2 The 4 Horns and the 4 Carpenters (ZECHARIAH 1:18-21)

Zechariah sees four horns, which have scattered Judah, Israel, and Jerusalem. The four carpenters cast them out to other nations. God's chosen people would reunite, and God would scorn those nations that brought sins and torment upon Israel.

3 A Man with a Measuring Line (ZECHARIAH 2:1-12)

A man measures the dimensions of the city of Jerusalem. An angel instructs Zechariah to tell the man the city will not need walls; God will protect it with a wall of fire. His presence will inhabit the city. This speaks to a time when Israel would be restored, and the Lord would be its protector.

4 Cleansing and Crowning Joshua (ZECHARIAH 3)

Joshua stands before the angel of the Lord in filthy clothing, and Satan is at his right hand. The angel orders clean clothes for him. This represents the cleansing of Israel and God's forgiveness. Joshua is crowned, and tasked with reestablishing a holy nation.

5 The Golden Candlestick and the 2 Olive Trees (ZECHARIAH 4)

Zechariah sees a golden candlestick with seven lamps and a bowl. Two olive trees flank the candlestick. Golden oil flows into the bowl. The lamps represent the eyes of God, ever-watchful; the trees represent the "two anointed ones." God would bring light and lift them from the darkness. The Messiah would ensure that Israel is the light of all nations.

6 The Flying Roll (ZECHARIAH 5:1-4)

A flying roll (scroll) represents the curse God will bring upon those who steal and take the Lord's name in vain. Those sinners will be cut off, and their houses will be destroyed. Zechariah is alluding to the judgments the Lord will bring upon Israel.

7 The Woman in an Ephah (Basket) (ZECHARIAH 5:5-11)

Zechariah lifts his eyes and sees a woman sitting in an ephah (a basket used to measure grain), representing wickedness. Two winged women appear, and they fly the basket up to heaven. This vision represents the removal of sin from Israel.

8 The 4 Chariots (ZECHARIAH 6:1-8)

The Four Horsemen of the Apocalypse descend from between two mountains of brass. The first chariot has red horses, the second has black, the third has white, and the fourth has bay. "These are the four spirits of the heavens, which go forth from standing before the Lord of all the earth." (ZECHARIAH 6:5) The horsemen represent the Lord's divine judgment, and His power to execute divine rule.

1 HOLY FIGURES ARE NOT IMMUNE FROM SIN.

The temple priests had been sacrificing imperfect animals—those that were sick, blind, deaf, lame, or otherwise disabled—with the reasoning that no one would notice, or care. In their apathy, the priests disrespected the Lord. Malachi urged the priests to repent, rectify their ways, and **"beseech God that he will be gracious unto us."** (MALACHI 1:9)

Who was Malachi?

- Last of the twelve Minor Prophets

- Wrote the final book in the Old Testament

- His name means "messenger" in Hebrew

2 FOLLOWERS MUST UPHOLD AND RESPECT THE LAWS OF MARRIAGE.

Malachi's prophecies spoke of the dangers of adultery and questioned the risks of pitting men against each other: **"Why do we deal treacherously every man against his brother, by profaning the covenant of our fathers?"** (MALACHI 2:10) He also cited the sins of the Israelites who married others of foreign religions. (MALACHI 2:11)

MALACHI'S
4 LESSONS
TO RESTORE THE COVENANT

His prophecies and lessons formed essential teachings for the Israelites—and helped them amend their sins and restore their covenant with the Lord.

3 GOD WILL JUDGE THE EVIL AND REWARD THE FAITHFUL.

Malachi reminded his people that those who commit evil acts will face God's wrath: **"I will come near to you to judgment; and I will be a swift witness against the sorcerers, and against the adulterers, and against false swearers, and against those that oppress."** (MALACHI 3:5) Those who fear the Lord, offer tithes, and uphold the covenant will be blessed. (MALACHI 4:2)

4 GOD WILL PREPARE THE ISRAELITES FOR THE MESSIAH.

Malachi promised the Israelites that he would send the prophet Elijah to prepare them for the coming of the Lord, the Messiah. (MALACHI 4:5) In preparation for His arrival, Elijah would purify the hearts of the Israelites: **"he shall turn the heart of the fathers to the children, and the heart of the children to their fathers."** (MALACHI 4:6)

THE NEW COVENANT

Much of God's Word in the Old Testament has to do with the covenant He made with the Israelites. His promise to the Israelites—that they would be His chosen people—depended upon their adherence to Mosaic Law. However, in the Old Testament, several prophets allude to a New Covenant, one that would be fulfilled through Jesus' life, death, and resurrection. The New Covenant is discussed even as God and the Israelites upheld the old. Moses, Jeremiah, and Ezekiel are three prophets who explicitly mention the New Covenant in their addresses to the people of Israel.

PROPHET

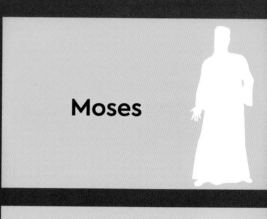

Moses

Jeremiah

Ezekiel

PREDICTION	FULFILLMENT
Foresees Israel failing to uphold the original covenant but predicts a time of forgiveness and restoration. (DEUTERONOMY 30:1-8)	Alludes to the New Covenant in one of his final declarations. Israel would be given a **"heart to perceive, and eyes to see, and ears to hear." (DEUTERONOMY 29:4)**
Predicts the Lord will create a New Covenant with the houses of Israel and Judah. "I will put my law in their inward parts, and write it in their hearts; and will be their God." (JEREMIAH 31:33)	The Messiah fulfills the prophecies. In MATTHEW 5:17, Jesus has come to fulfill God's law. The New Covenant would be written on the Israelites' hearts. By accepting Christ, they would enter the New Covenant with God.
Describes a New Covenant that will be written in the Israelites' hearts. The Holy Spirit would dwell within them. "A new heart also will I give you, and a new spirit will I put within you." (EZEKIEL 36:26)	New Testament verses confirm Ezekiel's predictions. The Israelites would no longer be under law, but under God's grace. (ROMANS 6:14) Jesus would make a New Covenant with the people. (HEBREWS 7:22)

HABAKKUK:
The Mysterious Prophet

Little is known about Habakkuk's life, family, or place of origin. However, he has an entire book of the Bible devoted to his dialogue with God.

HABAKKUK IS

8TH

OF THE 12 MINOR PROPHETS OF ISRAEL

THE OTHERS:
1. Hosea
2. Joel
3. Amos
4. Obadiah
5. Jonah
6. Micah
7. Nahum
8. **Habakkuk**
9. Zephaniah
10. Haggai
11. Zechariah
12. Malachi

- Habakkuk is mentioned by name only twice in the Bible.

- Habakkuk's name is loosely translated as "He that embraces."

- It is estimated that the Book of Habakkuk was written around 607 B.C.

- It is the 35th book of the Bible and the 13th of the 17 Books of Prophecy (Isaiah–Malachi).

- Habakkuk is the only prophet to devote his entire work to the question of the justice of God's government of the world.

- The Book of Habakkuk can be divided into three parts: a discussion between God and Habakkuk, an oracle of woe, and a psalm.

- Habakkuk's book is often considered to be a lesson in patience.

- The last word in the Book of Habakkuk is "instruments."

5

ENIGMATIC OLD TESTAMENT CHARACTERS

Big-name characters and their narratives dominate the Old Testament. The stories of Abraham, Noah, and Moses are well known to biblical scholars and laypeople alike. The Old Testament has many lesser-known—but still very important—characters who respond in faith to the Lord, and thereby show what life was like for God's covenant people in ancient times. Here is a deeper look at five obscure and enigmatic Old Testament characters.

1 Jethro

Jethro was Moses' father-in-law, and was a pillar of support when Moses became overwhelmed while leading the Israelites. In EXODUS 18, Moses expressed how beleaguered he was, tasked with making all of the decisions, settling all disputes, and answering all of his people's questions. Jethro suggested a remedy to ease Moses' burdens: divide the responsibilities between rulers of thousands, hundreds, fifties, and tens, so that smaller matters can be settled without overburdening Moses, and to maintain peace among the people. Moses followed Jethro's advice, and established a hierarchy of leadership to rule the people of Israel.

2 Naaman

Naaman was a Syrian captain. In 2 KINGS 5 he is described as honorable, mighty, and valiant—but he also suffered from leprosy. An Israelite servant suggested that Naaman journey to Israel to be healed by a prophet. Naaman traveled to Israel and met the prophet Elisha, who instructed him to wash in the Jordan River seven times. Naaman was angered (he expected a direct miracle from God), but the servant convinced him to obey, and he was healed. Naaman accepted the Israelites' God as his own, and brought the Lord's Word back to Syria. In a related story, Gehazi, a servant of Elisha, falsely obtained clothing and silver from Naaman. God punished Gehazi for his theft and deceit: Gehazi was struck with Naaman's leprosy, and his descendants were cursed with the disease as well!

3 Sherah

Sherah is briefly mentioned in the Old Testament, tucked away in 1 CHRONICLES 7. This entire chapter is dedicated to the genealogy of Issachar, and names all of his sons and their descendants. Though it was common to trace family lineage through men, it is interesting to note that in this history, Sherah is remembered for building the cities of Upper and Lower Bethhoron, and Uzzensherah (taking her name). Sherah must have been a very powerful and influential woman to build and lead cities in the male-dominated ancient world.

4 Og

Few details are provided about Og in the Old Testament, despite being mentioned several times in Deuteronomy. Og was a giant, and the King of Bashan. DEUTERONOMY 3 tells of a great battle between Israel and Og, in which God delivers Og and his people into the hands of the Israelites. Og is described as being one of the last descendants of the giants (the Rephaim), and the verses give an idea of his size. His bed was 9 cubits long by 4 cubits wide, or 13½ feet long by 6 feet wide!

5 Balaam

Balaam the prophet is described in NUMBERS 22. He is remembered for a rather odd reason: his donkey spoke to him! The King of Moab, Balak, sent Balaam to curse the Israelites and their lands. But God protected the Israelites, and sent the angel of the Lord to stop him. Balaam was blind to the angel, but his donkey saw it several times along their journey, repeatedly stopping in its tracks. Balaam was enraged at the delays, and whipped the animal because of it. The Lord opened the donkey's mouth to speak to Balaam, and asked why it was being beaten. In doing so, the Lord also opened Balaam's eyes to his sins.

6 LITTLE-KNOWN WOMEN OF THE OLD TESTAMENT

1. Noah's Wife

VERSE: Genesis 7

MAJOR ACCOMPLISHMENT: Played a crucial role during the flood, ensuring the Israelites' survival after the waters ebbed.

LONG-TERM EFFECT: Her presence upheld the Lord's covenant with His people.

2. Shiphrah and 3. Puah

VERSE: Exodus 1

MAJOR ACCOMPLISHMENT: Hebrew midwives during the time of Israeli enslavement in Egypt, Shiphrah and Puah disobeyed the Pharaoh's order to kill all male Hebrew babies at birth.

LONG-TERM EFFECT: The Hebrew population continued to grow and thrive despite their persecution by the Pharaoh, because a new generation of males survived.

4. The Woman of Thebez

VERSE: Judges 9

MAJOR ACCOMPLISHMENT: Abimelech, a Philistine warrior, led gruesome battles against the Israelites. Abimelech was confronted by a "certain woman" (JUDGES 9:53), who dropped a piece of millstone on his head, cracking his skull.

LONG-TERM EFFECT: The Woman of Thebez was an instrument of God used to stop Abimelech from destroying her city. The battle ended abruptly after Abimelech fell, ushering in forty-five years of peace for Israel.

Though they are not always given as much attention as the male protagonists of the Bible, there are many important and fascinating women discussed in the Old Testament. Some of the women are not even named, but their stories prove essential in the lives of many major biblical figures, showing that God has a purpose for all of His followers, and emphasizing the connectedness of all the faithful.

5. The Witch of Endor

VERSE: 1 Samuel 28

MAJOR ACCOMPLISHMENT: The Witch of Endor saw the spirits of the dead, and communicated a message from the ghost of Samuel to King Saul. After Samuel's death, Saul sought guidance for the impending conflict with the Philistines, and traveled in disguise to the Witch. The voice of Samuel criticized Saul for disobeying God, and predicted defeat and death. Saul's fate was carried out the next day; he committed suicide after losing the battle.

LONG-TERM EFFECT: The Witch of Endor is the catalyst for a pivotal moment in Israel's history: Saul's death made way for the rise of King David. Saul met his demise due to his continued defiance of the Lord—a reminder of the importance of following God's commands.

6. Rizpah

VERSE: 2 Samuel 3:7; 21:8–14

MAJOR ACCOMPLISHMENT: A concubine of King Saul, Rizpah became a victim of King David, who sought restitution for Saul's slaughter of the Gibeonites. As punishment, David ordered Rizpah's sons be killed: "they hanged them in the hill before the Lord." (2 SAMUEL 21:9) Rizpah protected the bodies until the rains poured down (signaling the Lord's forgiveness). Upon learning what Rizpah had done, David allowed the sons a proper burial.

LONG-TERM EFFECT: Rizpah's story is an example of the strength that faith in God brings. Rizpah's actions stress the importance of honoring the dead.

THE TOP 5 OLD TESTAMENT VILLAINS

1 The Serpent

In GENESIS 3, Satan came to the Garden of Eden in the form of a snake to challenge Adam and Eve, and to tempt them to disobey God. The Serpent told Eve to eat from the tree of knowledge of good and evil. It told her that by eating the fruit of the tree, she and Adam would be like the Lord, knowing good and evil. Eve ate from the tree, and gave some to Adam as well, an act now described as Original Sin. By their fall, the Serpent was able to bring about shame, punishment, fear, blame, and the knowledge of our own mortality.

2 Cain

Cain was a son of Adam and Eve, and is known as the first murderer in the Old Testament. His story is presented in GENESIS 4. Resentful of his younger brother, Abel, whom the Lord favored, Cain led Abel into a field, and murdered him in a fit of rage and jealousy. When confronted by the Lord, Cain denied his actions and lied to God. For this act of fratricide, Cain was cursed to wander the world alone.

3 Pharaoh

The Pharaoh was a constant oppressor of the Israelites, as told in EXODUS 5 and 7–9. He kept them enslaved in Egypt, despite the Lord's commands to free them. Because of his defiance, God brought ten plagues upon Egypt, which culminated in the death of all the firstborn Egyptian children and livestock. Even after the Pharaoh agreed to free the Israelites, he rescinded his word and sent his army after them. But the Pharaoh's command had dire consequences for Egypt. While pursuing the Israelites, the Egyptian army was destroyed as it crossed the Red Sea, and all of the soldiers were killed.

Goliath

In 1 SAMUEL 17, the David and Goliath narrative introduces us to Goliath, a giant Philistine warrior who stirred deep feelings of terror in the hearts of the Israelites. Israel was at war with the Philistines, again facing the enslavement of its people should it lose. The Philistines' top soldier, Goliath, stood at 9 feet tall, covered in armor, and mocked and frightened his foes for forty days on the battlefront. Despite his formidable size and power, it was the young David who took him down with a slingshot and a single stone. David then took Goliath's own sword, and chopped off his head.

4

The Old Testament is filled with heroic stories about underdogs who followed the Lord with deep faith, and frequently in the face of adversity. There are also the narratives that tell about those who disobeyed the Word of God. These "villains" range from a pagan queen to Satan himself, and they show us how to recognize and avoid evil, and to turn instead to trust in the Lord and His guidance. Here are some of the most notorious figures presented in the Old Testament.

5

Jezebel

Jezebel was a Queen of Israel who persuaded her husband, King Ahab, to worship the false gods Baal and Asherah. In defiance of the Lord, the priestess of Baal encouraged not just idolatry, but also human sacrifice, which came in the form of her followers' own children. She also was a murderer: Jezebel orchestrated the murders of the true prophets of Israel (1 KINGS 18:13); planned to assassinate the prophet Elijah (1 KINGS 19:2); and conspired to have a vineyard owner stoned to death so her husband could take the lands (1 KINGS 21). For her egregious sins, Jezebel was thrown out of a window and left to be eaten by stray dogs.

MINOR PROPHETS

As with the Major Prophets, the Minor Prophets were a conduit through which the Lord could speak to the Hebrews. They offered advice and guidance on all issues affecting the Israelites, and were living representations of how to follow and fear God's Word. In some, notably Haggai, prophecies can be dated to the year and month (even day) when they were uttered.

MAJOR PROPHETS

It is important to note that "Major" refers to the quantity of text in these books, and does not imply that these prophets are more important than those categorized as "Minor." These prophets often offered promise alongside rebuke and warning in times of great crisis in the Old Testament. They spoke on behalf of the Lord, and gave the Israelites a glimpse into the future, detailing what God had in store for them. Prophecy does not primarily mean "foretelling" (or predicting) so much as it signifies a "forthtelling" (telling forth) of what God wills.

MINOR PROPHETS

JOEL
AMOS
OBADIAH
JONAH
MICAH
NAHUM
HABAKKUK
ZEPHANIAH
HAGGAI
ZECHARIAH
MALACHI

MAJOR PROPHETS

ISAIAH
JEREMIAH
LAMENTATIONS
EZEKIEL
DANIEL

JOSHUA
JUDGES
RUTH
1 SAMUEL

UNDERSTANDING the Books

LAW

GENESIS
EXODUS
LEVITICUS
NUMBERS
DEUTERONOMY

POETRY & WISDOM WRITINGS

JOB
PSALMS
PROVERBS
ECCLESIASTES
SONG OF SOLOMON

HISTORY

ESTHER
NEHEMIAH
EZRA
2 CHRONICLES
1 CHRONICLES
2 KINGS
1 KINGS
2 SAMUEL

LAW (Torah or the Pentateuch)

The first five books of the Bible are commonly referred to either as the Pentateuch, or as the Torah, the books of the Law. Ascribed to Moses, these books are the Hebrews' most respected and holy scriptures, and are remembered as the first scriptures for the Israelites. Laws explained in these books include moral and practical precepts, as well as teachings relating to making sacrifices to God.

POETRY AND WISDOM WRITINGS

Ancient Hebrew poetry could rely on rhyme, rhythm, or meter, but also features extensive parallelism, imagery, and figures of speech to convey lessons and explain dramatic stories. Among many of the prominent themes of wisdom literature: the root of good and evil, human suffering, the nature of wisdom, trust in God, and the meaning of life.

HISTORY

The historical books present the history of the Israelites, the building and destruction of their lands and people, and their relationship (good and bad) with the Lord over the years. The stories describe how obedience to God's Word yielded blessings, and deviation from the covenant resulted in curses and punishment.

of the OLD TESTAMENT

POETRY AND WISDOM WRITINGS

MAJOR PROPHETS

MINOR PROPHETS

Understanding
HEAVEN

Throughout the Old Testament, there are many references to heaven, and taken together, they offer readers a glimpse into the magnitude of heaven, and a way of understanding life after death. Some Old Testament writers allude to their expectation of being in God's presence after their death (JOB 19:26 states, "in my flesh shall I see God"). According to DANIEL 12:2, there would be a general resurrection of the dead—"many of them that sleep" would awaken, some to "everlasting life," and others to "everlasting contempt."

EZEKIEL 36:35
In the Greek translation of the Old Testament (Septuagint) used by the earliest Christians, the word *paradise* is used not just to mean a pleasant garden (an original meaning of the word). It now also means either Eden, or a restored Eden—and by extension, heaven itself. Jesus said to one of the thieves who was crucified with him, "To day shalt thou be with me in paradise." (Luke 23:43) Paradise was a calming, peaceful location.

PSALM 86:13
Heaven can be understood simply as a place of deliverance, or a place where souls are spared from the depths and despairs of hell. Souls are saved according to God's mercy and forgiveness.

GENESIS 28

Jacob dreamed of a ladder that reaches heaven from the earth. In his dream, Jacob beheld "the angels of God ascending and descending on it." When he woke up, Jacob understood that the Lord was with him, and that the ladder represented the gates of heaven.

GENESIS 11

This chapter tells of a time when the Israelites believed they could reach heaven *without* needing the Lord to get there. They built a tower to reach heaven directly, but God stopped their progress, showing that one must follow the Lord to earn His favor in life after death.

PSALM 16

Heaven is also described as being at God's "right hand." Psalm 16 states that those who favor and follow the Lord are at His right hand, and their souls will not be abandoned to suffer in hell.

PSALM 23

This chapter describes heaven as the "house of the Lord." Some believe the reference is to the temple—which was for Jews the meeting place of heaven and earth. Traditionally, Psalm 23 has meant more than this to both Jews and Christians—the real hope of heaven—for those who believe the Lord to be their shepherd will not fear evil, even in death, since God will always be with them. Those who believe in God and follow His Word will "dwell in the house of the Lord for ever."

DANIEL 2:44

The Book of Daniel compares heaven to a "kingdom"—one that cannot and will not be destroyed. This kingdom will "stand for ever."

Comprehending
HELL

Old Testament references to hell paint a bleak picture of the eternal destination of sinners. The icons presented here will help in understanding the consequences of sin and rejecting the Lord's Word.

ISAIAH 14:15

The Hebrew word for the underworld can be translated to mean "THE PLACE OF THE DEAD" OR "A PIT." Isaiah 14:15 says, "Yet thou shalt be brought down to hell, to the sides of the pit." In these verses, hell opens itself to all men.

ISAIAH 66:24

This verse provides a horrifying description of death for those who transgressed against the Lord. It details how those SINNERS WILL SUFFER IN FIRES THAT CANNOT BE EXTINGUISHED, and their bodies will forever be eaten by worms that will not die.

The concept of hell is described in much further detail in the New Testament. Jesus references the torments of hell in His teachings, and His disciples warn the faithful of eternal punishment in hell. MATTHEW 10:28 warns of the destruction of "both soul and body in hell"; LUKE 16:23 describes those in hell as "being in torments"; and 2 PETER 2:4 describes how God did not save the angels that sinned against Him: He "cast them down to hell, and delivered them into chains of darkness."

DANIEL 12:2
This verse foresees a general resurrection of both the righteous and the unrighteous, and that those who rejected God will awake in the afterlife to "SHAME AND EVERLASTING CONTEMPT."

PSALM 55, PSALM 86, AND PROVERBS 7
In the Old Testament, hell is often described as a place that sinners "go down" to after they die. Psalm 55 states that the wicked will "GO DOWN QUICK INTO HELL"; Psalm 86 references being delivered from "the lowest hell"; and Proverbs 7 describes "going down to the chambers of death."

PSALM 9:17
Hell is often simply described as A PLACE WHERE THE WICKED DWELL: "The wicked shall be turned into hell, and all the nations that forget God."

Christian interpreters of the Old Testament have generally understood that those who died before the death and resurrection of Jesus awaited Christ's atoning sacrifice, and that His work on the cross opened heaven to them. For example, MATTHEW 27:52 tells how "the graves were opened; and many bodies of the saints which slept arose." But for the unbelievers, their spirits went to hell. "The angels shall come forth, and sever the wicked from among the just, and shall cast them into the furnace of fire; there shall be wailing and gnashing of teeth" (MATTHEW 13:49–50)

5 PREDICTIONS OF THE COMING OF JESUS

1 Eve's descendant will crush the serpent.
GENESIS 3:15

In this rather cryptic verse, God tells Eve that one of her descendants will crush the head of the serpent—Satan. It is Jesus himself who will completely triumph over evil. (Later, ROMANS 16:20 predicts that the Lord will "bruise Satan under your feet.")

2 God "shall dwell in the tents of Shem."
GENESIS 9:27

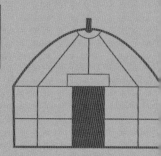

To Christians, this verse offers a prediction that the Lord will live among the Semites (Jewish people). Jesus is born to a Jewish family, and lives, teaches, and preaches among the Jews.

3 Jesus will arise from Jacob's family tree.
NUMBERS 24:17

"I shall see him, but not now: I shall behold him, but not nigh: there shall come a Star out of Jacob, and a Sceptre shall rise out of Israel." Jesus, the Messiah, would be a descendant of Jacob.

Jesus' birth, life, death, and resurrection are described in the New Testament. But Christians from the earliest days have understood much of the scripture in the Old Testament to make references to His coming, and to allude to his presence in the world, even before His birth. Here, a few predictions in the Old Testament—both cryptic and direct—reference the coming of the Messiah.

4 Mary will become the Mother of God.
ISAIAH 7:14

"Therefore the Lord himself shall give you a sign; Behold, a virgin shall conceive, and bear a son, and shall call his name Immanuel." This is one of the most direct lines referencing the Virgin Mary, and the birth of her son, Jesus, and is also cited in MATTHEW 1:23.

5 The Messiah will reign supreme across the world. ISAIAH 9:6

"For unto us a child is born, unto us a son is given: and the government shall be upon his shoulder: and his name shall be called Wonderful, Counsellor, The mighty God, The everlasting Father, The Prince of Peace." The verses continue, describing how Jesus will sit upon the throne of David, and He will bring perpetual peace to the land. The gospel writer Luke depends on these words in his famous telling of Christ's birth. (LUKE 2:11)

APPENDIX:
Books of the Old Testament, KJV (King James Version)

There are thirty-nine books in the Old Testament. You'll find a summary of each one of them in this appendix, so you can get a snapshot of some of their most important themes and lessons.

Genesis: Genesis addresses basic questions—how did the world and all that is in it come into being? It also tells how God shaped Israel, and called all humanity by means of a covenant; namely He promises land, nation, and children, in exchange for our obedience.

Exodus: Exodus tells how God delivered the Israelites from slavery in Egypt and their forty-year sojourn in the wilderness before entering the Promised Land. God calls them to faithful obedience to His law (epitomized in but not limited to Ten Commandments).

Leviticus: Leviticus consists of God's instructions to Moses on how Israel is to worship Him, what "uncleanness" is (usually a state in which a thing, person, or animal is unfit to be brought into the presence of God in worship), and how a person can be purified to worship. Key themes include atonement (how human beings can make up for sin by looking not to themselves but to God) and just what holiness is (the "holiness code").

Numbers: Numbers takes its name from a census of the Israelites gathered at Mount Sinai, but also goes on to tell the history of their forty years of wandering in the wilderness, largely brought about by their sinful disobedience to God's calling.

Deuteronomy: Deuteronomy consists of three speeches of Moses to the Israelites, who are still in the wilderness but soon to enter the Promised Land. The speeches call them to obedience to God's law, and promise God's care to an observant and repentant nation.

Joshua: Joshua is Moses' successor, after Moses is not permitted by God to enter the Promised Land. Joshua is victorious in the conquest of the land. At the end, he calls Israel to "choose you this day whom ye will serve" (meaning, avoid false worship).

Judges: Judges tells how in Israel's earliest years, certain rulers (called "Judges") held the leadership instead of a king (God is to be king of kings). Vivid, fast-paced narratives about individual Judges weave a theme of disobedience of, and then return to, God.

Ruth: Ruth is a short book named after a Moabite woman married to an Israelite living in Moab. When he dies, she follows his mother back to Israel ("thy people shall be my people") and God blesses her. She comes to represent other non-Jewish nations, and she foreshadows Christ's coming, as she is among Jesus' mother's ancestors.

1 Samuel: 1 Samuel describes how Israel desires to be like "all the other nations" that have a king. Recognizing their continued disobedience without a king, God reluctantly allows it. Through His prophet Samuel, God makes His choice clear: Saul is called to be Israel's first king. In many respects, he will be a disappointment, to both God and the people.

2 Samuel: 2 Samuel relates how David becomes king in place of Saul, and how God promises an "eternal covenant" with David and his lineage. For Christians, the eternal covenant prefigures the New Covenant established by the coming of Jesus, whose mother is a lineal descendant of David's.

1 Kings: 1 Kings is the narrative of David's son and successor as king, Solomon. Solomon has fabled wisdom—for which he had prayed, instead of for wealth or power. But Solomon, and even more, his sons, turn away from faithful obedience, and the kingdom is divided into two kingdoms, Israel and Judah.

2 Kings: 2 Kings continues a narrative on the great prophet Elijah and his successor, Elisha. It also summarizes the deeds of good kings like Hezekiah and Josiah, as well as wicked ones like Manasseh. The book closes with the fall of Jerusalem to the Babylonians.

1 Chronicles: 1 Chronicles begins with a genealogy of the descendants of Adam. It then largely parallels the 1 Kings narrative up through the kingship of David, but from the perspective of the southern kingdom.

2 Chronicles: 2 Chronicles picks up the narrative with Solomon on the throne, and details the divided kingdom (north and south) after his death and the events leading to the destruction of Jerusalem at the hands of the Babylonians.

Ezra: Ezra begins with the decree of Cyrus the Persian freeing the Israelites from their Babylonian captivity, and their return to Jerusalem to rebuild the city and temple. Ezra continually warns Israel against the syncretism it foresees in intermarriage with non-Jews.

Nehemiah: Nehemiah is a first-person account of an Israelite living in Persia who returns to Jerusalem as its governor and supervises the rebuilding of the city walls. In addition to physical renovations, Nehemiah reads the Mosaic law to the Israelites and acts as a reformer.

Esther: Esther is the account of a Jewish woman living in Persia, probably during the fifth century B.C. She marries the Persian king, and skillfully uses her position at court to head off the killing of Jews in Persia by the evil Haman.

Job: Job is about a good man beset by successive tragedies planned by Satan to show God that even the righteous can be deflected from faith. Job's friends urge him to confess any hidden sin, which they presume to be behind his calamities. In Job's dialogue with God, he is reminded of a sovereign plan hidden to human eyes.

Psalms: Psalms is a collection of 150 worship songs—the hymnbook of ancient Israel. Praises, laments, pilgrimage, and kingship songs of varying length, the psalms were used in temple worship, and continually call Israel to righteous obedience and radical trust.

Proverbs: Proverbs is an anthology of sayings about life, faith, and wisdom. Wisdom (personified as a "she") was present and active in the earth's creation. Proverbs's themes include the idea that "the fear of the Lord is the beginning of knowledge," a sharp contrast between wisdom and folly, and the encouragement to pursue wisdom as the goal of faithful life.

Ecclesiastes: Ecclesiastes, ascribed to Solomon, refers to its narrator as "the preacher." A principal theme is that all human endeavor is "vanity," and there is "no new thing under the sun." Life is simply to enjoy our work, food, and drink. At the end, the preacher says we are to "fear God, and keep His commandments." Is this not our chief purpose?

Song of Solomon: Song of Solomon (or sometimes, "Song of Songs") is the dialogue between two unidentified lovers. Beautifully written, the Song strongly evokes images of erotic love in a way that has been mostly understood as allegorical. Christians (including the Puritans) have often preached it as an allegory of Christ and the church, His bride.

Isaiah: Isaiah, named after the prophet to whom it is attributed, consists of sixty-six chapters. It prophesies God's judgment against those who have disobediently turned against Him. Yet even if a small group of people returns to the Lord, they will be saved. Great moments in Isaiah include the call of the prophet, and notably for Christians, the so-called "suffering servant" passages.

Jeremiah: Jeremiah prophesies during the period from Josiah's reforms up through the beginning of the Babylonian captivity. Starting with the prophet's call, the book is intensely personal. Prophecies are "enacted" and not just spoken (e.g., the wearing of an ox yoke to symbolize the coming captivity of Israelites in Babylon). Jeremiah calls people to return to faith and notably promises a "new covenant" in the heart.

Lamentations: Lamentations is traditionally ascribed to Jeremiah. Its five chapters, each of them a separate lament, grieve the destruction of Jerusalem. The book raises the possibility that God has finally rejected Israel completely. But interestingly, the book is also famous for saying, "His compassions fail not."

Ezekiel: Ezekiel begins with a spellbinding vision of God riding in a chariot drawn by four living creatures: man, lion, ox, and eagle. God is also glimpsed in a vision, seated on a throne and leaving the temple because of its idolatrous practices. Other notable visions include that of the dry bones (Israel being revived) and a new temple and city.

Daniel: Daniel's revelation of the end times (apocalypse) is itself set in the period when Israel is beginning its Babylonian captivity. One of the exiled Israelites, and steadfast in his faith, Daniel interprets the Persian king's dreams—the dream of four kingdoms, the tree cut down, creatures from the sea, and the ram and the goat. Perhaps the most famous one is Daniel's interpretation of the king's dream at Belshazzar's feast.

Hosea: Hosea is told by God to marry a prostitute, Gomer. In her infidelity, she represents Israel, which has been similarly unfaithful to its covenant with God. Hosea and Gomer subsequently divorce (possibly representing division in Israel between south and north), and then they remarry. Hope is held out for Israel's ultimate redemption.

Joel: Joel prophesies the end times with the terrifying prospect of a swarm of locusts consuming all crops and a great army upon the mountains. Yet the prophecy holds out hope for Israel, as God pours out His Spirit of redemption and restoration. All nations will be judged; Jerusalem will be inhabited forever.

Amos: Amos, a native of Judah, preaches to the northern kingdom in Israel. He forecasts God's coming judgment upon Israel's neighbors, Damascus, Tyre, Edom, and Moab, but also upon Judah and Israel. He despises Israel's sacrifices: "let judgment run down as waters." Locusts, fire, and a plumb line (a carpenter's tool used to determine the vertical on an upright surface) are shown to Israel, but at the end, redemption is offered.

Obadiah: Obadiah has a vision of the fall of Edom, Israel's neighbor, originally settled by patriarch Jacob's brother Esau. Some interpret Edom, however, to be representative of all nations that have persecuted Israel.

Jonah: Jonah goes to sea to elude God's call to preach to despised Nineveh. A storm overtakes the ship, and its crew throw Jonah overboard because they see their peril as the result of him fleeing God. Swallowed by a great fish, he comes up out of it onto land, and goes to Nineveh. The city repents, but Jonah is angry. God asks, "should not I spare Nineveh?"

Micah: Micah believes ruin and destruction are coming upon Israel for its evil. Yet, God will gather up a "remnant." Nations will come upon the mountain of the Lord, and Israel will be freed from Babylon. A ruler will come up out of Bethlehem. What does God require but that we "do justly, and to love mercy and to walk humbly with thy God?"

Nahum: Nahum says that God is against Nineveh for its oppression of Israel. Jerusalem should once again keep its feasts, in anticipation of restoration. Nineveh should prepare for an upcoming siege.

Habakkuk: Habakkuk foretells judgment upon Israel's enemies, the "Chaldeans" (Babylonians). If the vision (which was shown to the prophet) seems slow, Israel is to wait for it: "The just shall live by his faith."

Zephaniah: Zephaniah foretells that "the great day of the Lord is near." Israel's enemies will be judged, but Israel's evil will also be exposed. The nations will be punished and converted. The Lord sings and exults in a song of joy that closes the prophecy.

Haggai: Haggai prophesies during the same time period in which Ezra and Nehemiah are restoring the walls of Jerusalem and rebuilding its temple, after the restoration of Israel from its Babylonian captivity. If Israel is in want, it is because of its own slackness in rebuilding the temple. Still, the "glory of this latter house shall be greater than of the former."

Zechariah: Zechariah's end times prophecy begins with eight visions culminating in the hope that the nations of the world will become nothing less than God's kingdom. Israel is given encouragement that God will continue to bless it: "In that day shall the Lord defend the inhabitants of Jerusalem."

Malachi: Malachi declares that Israel's priests (the Levites) have been corrupt. God's messenger will prepare the way for His own coming to bring judgment. Judgment will be like the heat of a furnace—purifying Israel of its corruption. At the end of the book, the preaching of Moses is recalled and the coming of Elijah is promised.

ABOUT THE WRITER

Hillary Thompson is a freelance writer, editor, and researcher who studied history at Stonehill College and earned a master's degree in crime and justice studies at Suffolk University. After holding editorial positions in the publishing industry for eight years, Hillary now works full-time as a crime analyst for a local police department. When she isn't working, Hillary loves cooking, traveling, and renovating her nineteenth-century colonial. She lives in Brockton, Massachusetts.

ABOUT THE TECHNICAL REVIEWER

Edward Duffy has taught New Testament Greek language at Hartford Seminary since 2004. His PhD dissertation focused on an early Christian commentary on the Old Testament Book of Job, written in Greek during the fourth century A.D. by Didymus the Blind of Alexandria, Egypt. The commentary was lost to history until its discovery in the years just after World War II. An ordained pastor, he is the minister of First Presbyterian Church in Fairfield, Connecticut.

ABOUT THE DESIGNER

Erin Dawson is a highly caffeinated designer who has been making books for more than twenty years. She grew up in Southern Vermont before venturing over the border to study design and illustration at the Nova Scotia College of Art and Design. She now resides in the Berkshires with her husband and daughter.

ACKNOWLEDGMENTS

From Hillary

A sincere thank-you to: my friends at Adams Media for the opportunity to write this book. Pastor Edward Duffy, PhD, for his expertise, thoughtful edits, patience, and humor as we worked together on this great project. To my parents, for their support in everything I have worked to accomplish. To my sister Bee, for cooking, keeping the house, and keeping me sane during the long hours of research and writing. To Zack, for being the funniest man on earth. To my new family at the BPD. And most important, to my beautiful grandmother Doris Thompson. Her unwavering faith, strength, and grace surround and uplift everyone she meets.

From Ed

As I worked with the gifted and perceptive Hillary Thompson, trying to offer helpful feedback to her, I felt a great sense of gratitude to the teachers and mentors in my professional formation—most especially the almost legendary Bernhard Anderson of Princeton Theological Seminary, whose insights on the Hebrew Bible continue to inform mine. My greatest debt of gratitude will always go to my wife, Lynne, whose unconditional support and love make all things possible.

INDEX

Note: Page numbers in **bold** indicate references to summaries of books of the Old Testament.